"*Thy Word have I hid in mine heart*

Presented by the

Bible Memory Association
International
St. Louis, Missouri

To

JAMES L
WHITEMAN

AS A REWARD

for memorizing Scripture

in the annual Contest

that I might not sin against Thee."

M. R. DE HAAN

M. R.
DE HAAN

the
Man
and
His
Ministry

James R. Adair

ZONDERVAN
PUBLISHING HOUSE
Grand Rapids, Michigan

To Priscilla DeHaan
who loved him and whose graces,
as he stated in the dedication
of his first book, reminded
him daily of the reality
of the power of the Word
in Christian life.

FOREWORD

A book such as this would never have been written had my father been the one to make the decision. During his entire ministry he said little concerning his own life, and minimized the things others said about him which seemed to him to be self-glory.

Now that he has gone "Home" and his labors have ended, however, it is most fitting and proper that this volume be published, not to magnify a man, but to glorify God and to demonstrate what He can do through one who makes himself available.

God does accomplish His work through His children. He could have chosen special heavenly emissaries, but in supreme wisdom God made the very ones who have experienced His saving grace to be the channels through which the glorious news of redemption should be communicated. As in past ages chosen human vessels conveyed God's message, so today the Lord raises up men to speak to their generation. Such was John the Baptist, of whom the Bible says, "There was a *man* sent from God . . ." (John 1:6). My father also was a divinely appointed messenger, and in this biography you will see God at work through a *man*, one just as human as you or I, and subject to the same limitations and frailties. To recognize that the Lord uses human instruments in the fulfillment of His divine program should be an encouragement to every believer.

The memories I have of my father are precious. He was a man strong in spirit, with deep, uncompromising convictions. I can recall hearing him say, "I don't care if the *whole world* is against me, I must stand for what I believe is right." Yet, although firm and steadfast, he was known by his associates to be an unusually warm-hearted person, having an earnest compassion for others and a genuine love for his Lord. These are qualities which I would seek to emulate.

His faithful teaching of the Word of God, however, has made the greatest impression upon my life. When he was led into the ministry, and turned his back on the practice of medicine which he loved, this new and higher calling became his all-consuming passion. And, God honored his dedication.

I pray, as this volume is sent forth, that the life and ministry of my father will be used to lead many, especially the young in years, to take a firm stand upon the Word of God, and to make themselves available in His hands to do His bidding. God has His men for every generation. If just one should read these pages and through them be aroused into active service, then the "making of this book" shall not have been in vain. Rather, it will be another chapter in the ongoing ministry of M. R. DeHaan, M.D., a "man sent from God," who, "being dead, yet speaketh." Then even he would approve of this work, for he could say with the great apostle, ". . . they glorified God in me" (Galatians 1:24).

RICHARD W. DeHAAN
Grand Rapids, Michigan

ABOUT THIS BOOK

So far as I could determine Dr. M. R. DeHaan never told his fascinating story publicly — certainly not in detail. He didn't want the spotlight turned on him. His God-given message was what mattered, he often said.

I learned his attitude firsthand a number of years ago when I approached him following a church service and broached the idea of a biographical article for *Power*, a weekly publication which I edit; but he wasn't interested. Then in 1965 Dr. DeHaan died. A year ago, despite the good Doctor's coolness toward personal publicity, Radio Bible Class officials decided that the DeHaan story should be put in permanent form, to show how the power of God worked through a life. I was pleased when the Zondervan Publishing House, unaware of my earlier interest in Dr. DeHaan's story, asked me to write this book for the Radio Bible Class.

As I made numerous interviews and pored over clippings and other published material regarding the founder of the Radio Bible Class, I discovered Dr. DeHaan was indeed the colorful, godly person I had assumed him to be. Known to most listeners of Radio Bible Class only as a beloved, gravelly-voiced teacher, he was a man of great drive and brilliance, a leader of unusual spiritual depth and insight, a disciple as human as Simon Peter.

This volume does not pretend to deal in depth with all of the facets of the DeHaan story but mainly with those events and facts that Richard DeHaan and other Radio Bible Class officials believe will be of special interest and value to "Class members" and others who have followed the DeHaan ministry. According to Richard DeHaan, his late father's successor in the radio ministry, "The entire story would fill volumes. In this book on my father and his ministry, we hope to show how God led step by step in achieving His purpose."

I am indebted to many people who took of their time and shared information contained in this volume — members of the DeHaan family, the Radio Bible Class staff, longtime friends of Dr. DeHaan, and scores of others.

JAMES R. ADAIR
Wheaton, Illinois

CONTENTS

M. R.
DE HAAN

1

I have lent him to the Lord; as long as he liveth
he shall be lent to the Lord. . . . *1 Samuel 1:28*

Boy at a Street Meeting

A smile played at the corners of her thin, stern mouth and
tears of joy welled in her blue eyes that warm morning of
June 11, 1901, as Johanna DeHaan watched 15-year-old John,
her eldest son, leave for school. To her, there was no finer lad
in all the town of Zeeland, nor even elsewhere throughout
the surrounding Dutch colony. She dabbed her eyes with
her white apron, taking care that her younger sons, Ralph
and Martin, didn't see her and misunderstand her tears.
From a window of the two-story red brick home on the
corner of Lincoln and Peck Streets, Johanna, a plumpish
woman of 35, watched him disappear on his way toward
Zeeland High School on Main Street. Then she returned to

her kitchen chores, undoubtedly too preoccupied with thought to notice animals at play and birds flitting in the hemlocks and maples on the edge of the swamp back of the outhouse. It had all started last night as Johanna talked with her husband:

"Reitze, it's time we made some decision regarding John's further schooling. He's finishing ninth grade, and it's not too early for us to start planning how we'll send him to college." Reitze was the town cobbler, a gentle, practical man who wanted the best for his family, though he made not much more most of the time than a dollar a·day, hardly enough to assure each child a college education.

Johanna, who most certainly had more than an equal vote in family decisions, suggested they should tighten up even more on their spending, and begin looking into the matter of a loan for John's advanced schooling, likely at Hope College in nearby Holland.

By the light of a kerosene lamp, the DeHaans talked of the professions and occupations that John might study for. Businessman, lawyer, doctor, preacher. . . . Of course, only John himself, who had not yet said what he wanted to be, could really decide, they concluded. "How nice it would be if God called him to be a minister," mused Johanna. Reitze agreed that this would be the fulfillment of their dreams and prayers.

Before school that Tuesday morning, June 11, Johanna had shared with John the news that they were definitely planning to send him to college.

His face brightened and he looked past his mother out the window as if trying to penetrate the future. "Let's see; I'm 15 now and by the time I'm 22, the Lord willing, I will be a minister."

The words sent an electric tingle down Johanna's spine, and these were the words she pondered as John rode his bike toward Zeeland High.

That afternoon, following school, John DeHaan and a friend, Herman Boone, rode their bikes to a lakelike stretch

16

of the Black River west of Zeeland called Boone's River. With other school friends, they gathered water lilies for botany class. The fun was over and the others were starting home when John and Herman called, "There are some nicer lilies out there; we're going to stay and get them. We'll catch up with you on our bikes."

What happened after that was never fully known. Harry and Thomas Vander Pels, of Zeeland, who were fishing, saw them picking water lilies about 4:45 o'clock. As they left to fish farther upstream, the two boys were stripping for a swim. About 6:30 the two men returned to the spot where the boys had been and noticed their clothes on the river bank but they were gone. Struck with the thought that possibly they had drowned, the fishermen began raking the bottom of the river with their cane poles. Within fifteen minutes they discovered both bodies in about six feet of water and about six feet apart.

For Johanna and Reitze DeHaan, the dream of having their eldest son become a minister had been shattered within a few hours. The gentle, shimmering Black River had become a slithering, greedy monster, snuffing out the lives of the two teenagers. And John's words that had thrilled Johanna's heart were to linger only as memories and suggest what might have been.

Yet the Lord could choose either Ralph, the next oldest, or little Martin to take John's place. But neither showed the inclinations that John had exhibited. John had taken great interest in attending services with the family at the First Christian Reformed Church, and had taken catechism classes seriously.

Eleven-year-old Ralph also gave himself seriously to things of the church, but he was quiet and somewhat of an introvert, likely not the type God would call to the ministry. Ten-year-old Martin, on the other hand, was more extrovertish and earthy, the kind of lad more interested in Crackerjacks (and the prize inside the box), and frogs,

17

pollywogs, and skunks . . . and following the town lamp-lighter from corner to corner of an evening. While, of course, he was still young, he didn't sense the importance of prayer.

When a visiting minister was asked at the dinner table by his father to offer thanks for the food, Martin had embarrassed his parents with, "Could you please make it short, so we can get on with the meal?"

But there came a day when, at least to Martin, it seemed that God's hand had touched him in a special way.

Periodically the slow clop, clop of horses' hoofs and the creaking of a buckboard wagon moving into town from the west and carrying a tall woman evangelist brought swarms of young Hollanders to Main Street. Martin was often among them. Dressed in wide-collared shirts, short corduroy pants or knickers, long stockings and high-top shoes, they scampered from white frame and red brick houses with steep gabled roofs and skinny windows to taunt the woman with the thundering voice who preached from the buckboard. Her name was Nellie Churchford and she came from the City Mission in Holland. She was a sort of female John the Baptist, emerging as she did from the wilderness that separated the two towns and preaching a coming judgment on those not found in Jesus Christ. Up and down Main Street her powerful voice reverberated from store fronts with clear statements on how to escape God's wrath:

"Salvation is all of God's grace. You don't earn it by baptism, catechism, or church membership! You don't inherit it from your parents. Confess your sin and be born again by Jesus Christ into the family of God!"

She quoted proof texts like, "For by grace are ye saved through faith; and that not of yourselves, it is the gift of God — Not of works, lest any man should boast" (Ephesians 2:8, 9).

Ignoring the taunts of youngsters, Nellie stood tall, probably wearing a black full-skirted, ankle-length dress with a high lace collar and fitted, long-sleeved blouse. She shook

18

her long index finger at the Zeelanders, hoping the Truth would sink deeply into the hearts of some of her listeners.

It was when he was about 12 that Martin felt as if the long, thin finger of Nellie Churchford had singled him out as the worst sinner in town. That day he didn't jeer with the rest of the kids, neither did he let on to anyone that the message had spoken to him. But as the buckboard creaked back toward Holland, with Nellie's husband at the reins, he trudged homeward, serious, important thoughts bombarding his boyish mind and heart. Sometime that afternoon, likely in his room, 12-year-old Martin talked to God as never before. By faith, he wanted to be saved and be the kind of Christian Nellie Churchford talked about. He apparently didn't discuss it in detail with his parents, or friends, nor rush out to tell his pastor what he had done. This, he felt, was personal — between God and him. And, besides, those he knew would have thought him presumptuous to talk about being saved. Most good church-going Hollanders of that day hoped they were saved but they didn't think anyone could know for sure.

It's not clear that Martin had a genuine spiritual experience at this time; no marked change came into his life, though in later life he made occasional reference to the happening. Whether becoming a minister entered his mind isn't known either. Often when a boy comes face to face with the Eternal, he does have such thoughts. If he had, and had broken the news, it would not only have pleased his godly parents but friends as well. For they were all hard-working, God-fearing people who delighted to see their sons become men of the church.

Zeeland, as well as all the Dutch colony of which it was a part, had a heritage deeply rooted in Christian faith. The founders of Zeeland, like the seventeenth century Pilgrim separatists, had been men who traded persecution in the homeland for a fresh start and a life of hardship in America in order that they and their families might worship and serve

God according to their beliefs. They were perceptive, imaginative people from Zeeland, the most southerly maritime province of the Netherlands, rugged individualists who for centuries had fought the sea and whose motto was: *"Luctor et emergo"* (I struggled and I emerge).

Trouble for them had begun in the Netherlands after the Crown established the state church in 1816. Influenced by the radical liberal theology of contemporary German thought, the church had developed a spirit of reckless free thinking and a dead formalism. Finally, in 1834, a loud protest of many pastors and their congregations resulted in secession and the establishment of the "Christelijk Afgescheiden Kerk."

Persecution followed, though a royal decree in 1836 eased matters somewhat. In the ensuing years the abused separatists talked of emigration. In September 1846 Albertus Christiaan Van Raalte, an enthusiastic young minister of the secession, sailed from Rotterdam for the United States with his family and forty-seven followers. They settled in February 1847 in western Michigan, founding the city of Holland. Next a body of prospective colonists in Zeeland completed a church organization, called Cornelius Van Der Meulen to be their pastor-leader, and 457 of them sailed in the spring of 1847, also for the States. Such a move by an emigrating group — coming as a complete church — had not been known since the days of the Pilgrims.

On June 27, after many had died from hardship and disease, the homesick Zeelanders arrived on a flat boat at Van Raalte's Holland. Jannes Van De Luyster, who had been a wealthy land owner in the province of Zeeland, then set up headquarters six miles east of the Holland settlement and proceeded to buy land at $1.25 an acre for a village to be called Zeeland. In his journal, Van De Luyster recorded the reason for the name: "Because it was founded by the Zeelanders, who called upon the name of the Lord to prosper His work, and that His name might be called upon there forever."

The Zeelanders worshiped for the first time there, under Dominie Van Der Meulen, on the third Sunday in August 1847. Coached by those who had already conquered the wilderness, these Dutch settlers, with patience, perseverance, industry, and common sense, slashed out a rectangular village whose lots sold for $6.48 each. Here, for years to come, they would live under the able leadership of Jannes Van De Luyster, "the proprietor of the village of Zeeland," and Cornelius Van Der Meulen, the sympathetic, resourceful "Apostle of Zeeland."

Over the years stories of the advantages of living in the Dutch colony enticed more immigrants from the Netherlands, including 22-year-old Reitze DeHaan, who came to Zeeland in the fall of 1881. The same year 15-year-old Johanna Rozema, with several sisters and brothers, settled there.

In time Reitze became the town cobbler, but in those early years his thoughts were more on winning the hand of lovely Johanna than on mending shoes. A young man with an oval chin, a rather wide mouth, long sideburns, and oversized ears, he admired Johanna's industriousness and little, stubborn Dutch ways. There was nothing giddy about her and she loved the church as he did. Besides, there was much attractive about her: rather large blue eyes, a determined mouth, skin as delicate as a rose petal, and dark hair pulled tight and worn in a little knot; her figure pleased him, though she was ever so slightly taller than he was.

Reitze left his pedal stitcher and the smell of leather as he closed shop one day, and, with excitement surging within, hurried to ask Johanna the magic question. They were married in 1885, when she was 19 and he, 26. John was born a year later, followed in 1889 by a second son, Ralph.

Though Johanna longed for a girl, her third child, born on March 23, 1891, was another boy. She and Reitze decided he would be named after Reitze's brother, Martin, who worked with him at the cobbler's shop. The squalling

21

baby, who had come to live in the two-story red brick house on Lincoln Street, was given the full name, Martin Ralph. Little did Johanna and Reitze guess, then or even much later, that the lungy youngster would someday be a preacher, heard by radio around the world.

Marty was not quite ten when a daughter, Anna, was born to the DeHaans, but she died in infancy. Then a short time later a girl was added to the family through adoption. It was the day before Christmas 1901 that Wiebe Vander Velde lost his wife in childbirth, and found that five children were too much for him to handle. The baby, Peter, went to relatives; three-year-old Ada came to live with the DeHaans and was later legally adopted.

It is Ada (Mrs. Ada Middlehoek of Holland, Michigan) who recalls the sketchy details of Johanna DeHaan's day that began so happily and ended so tragically in the drowning of her would-be minister son, John. She was too young, of course, to remember the occurrence, but her mother related the story to her in later years. Her brother, Ralph, died in 1950 of complications following an automobile accident.

Ada recalls the day-and-night difference between Ralph and his younger brother, Marty. "Ralph didn't care about worms and bugs and things like that, as Marty did. Their natures were different and they didn't even look alike. Ralph was thinner-faced, and was a little taller. In temperament he took more after my dad while Mart took after Mother, who was higher strung than Dad."

Mart, his sister recalls, once embarrassed his mother because of his keen interest in the insect world. As a boy of perhaps seven or eight, he visited with Johanna in the home of a Hollander who was, as were many of the Dutch women, "crazy clean." Mrs. DeHaan herself kept her home spotless, brush-scrubbing woodwork and floor. And each spring and fall, she cleaned house thoroughly, including the washing and airing of all the bedding. But this woman went even further, washing the clothesline poles every week, and keeping her house almost antiseptically clean. Thus both women were horrified when they discovered that Marty had brought flies in his pocket and was releasing them one by one, until the house was buzzing with the pests.

In a real sense the holy Scriptures were the center of the DeHaan home, as in most of the homes of the area. With pious regularity Reitze read from the family Bible before each meal, followed by a substantial prayer, thanking God for supplying their needs and invoking His divine blessing. There was also a prayer of thanksgiving *after* every meal.

Around the table, there was a babel, with three languages being spoken. When Reitze talked with Johanna, it was usually in Frisian, their native dialect, a Low German tongue closely related to Anglo-Saxon. To the children the parents spoke Dutch, and the youngsters responded in English, which, of course, the parents understood but spoke with difficulty.

Meals in the home were not fancy — basically meat and potatoes. Dessert was an occasional treat, generally apple or pumpkin pie. When Ada grew old enough, she took over the cooking, done on a combination wood-gas range. Johanna's health became an increasing problem, making household chores difficult and calling for an extra amount of rest.

Thanksgiving and Christmas were the big holidays for the DeHaans. They didn't have a tree and did little decorating at Christmastime, but enjoyed exchanging gifts.

Like most other Zeelanders, the DeHaans were strict in their observance of Sunday. The parents regarded it as the Sabbath, holy unto God, and all weekday activities ceased. The children dared not even play in the yard. Sunday mornings the children were likely to awaken to the lusty voice of their father singing hymns and Dutch psalms as, with two fingers, he played the wheezy old reed organ downstairs.

The family faithfully attended church three times on Sundays — morning, afternoon, and evening — where the relatively long services were in the Dutch language. The children went to catechism classes on Tuesdays, and these, too, were in Dutch.

In the first sixteen years of married life, Reitze and Johanna were members of the First Christian Reformed Church, but following John's tragic death they soon left and placed their membership in the First Reformed Church. It seems that the minister of their church didn't come to see them to offer comfort and help, whereas the pastor of the First Reformed Church showed special kindness to the family. The Reformed Church dated back to the founding of Zeeland, its first pastor having been the good Dominie Van Der Meulen.

From time to time Martin would visit his father's cobbler shop, and chat with him and his Uncle Martin who was a man with fascinating ideas. Uncle Mart talked of his religious beliefs, ideas that weren't generally heard or appreciated around the Dutch community of Zeeland. He was considered to be sort of a heretic and took pleasure in it. Christ, he said, was going to return someday in bodily form, just as He had been received into heaven following His resurrection; He could come any day. Believers were to be taken up to be with Jesus — the dead were to be raised, and the living were to follow them to be forever with Him. After a seven-year tribulation period on earth, Christ, with many of His followers, would set up a thousand-year kingdom on earth, over which He would rule from Jerusalem, asserted Uncle Martin, who shared with his nephew proof of his beliefs from a well-worn Bible.

While Mart was enchanted, he didn't as a boy become a follower of Uncle Martin and his ideas. Instead, he had more interest in living in the here and now. He continued to be concerned with collecting insects, or looking for frogs along the edge of the cedar swamp out back of his house. He had a greater desire to study the habits of animals, or watch a bird in flight. Mart liked to explore and learn what life was all about.

24

He enjoyed talking with the fellows, though he was generally regarded a loner. There were sessions along the railroad tracks where they sat and discussed everything from the facts of life to theology. One boy from the gang ran away to Grand Rapids and returned with the story that he had heard a minister who seemed to doubt that the Bible was truly God's inspired Word — at least not all of it.

"We began to bat that around, and it was one of the most helpful discussions in this teenage period of my life," recalls D. J. De Pree, a boyhood friend of Martin DeHaan. "This conversation made us wonder if everything preached in our town was right. I don't definitely remember Martin in these conversations, but I imagine he was there. We had a gang and he was in it."

As a student, Martin was "one of the best students in the class," says De Pree. "I think it was quite general that students in our period took four years of Latin and two years of German. He did a minimum of homework and preparation, but our teacher, Miss Wilhelm, herself a German, was really impressed by the way he could stand up in class and give a free translation of German. Actually, he knew the Frisian language so well that when it came to German he had little problem, because of its similarity. This particularly appealed to the teacher."

Apparently Martin's keen mind was not as challenged as it might have been in school. Since occasionally he wasn't prepared with his lessons, he devised a standard trick to avoid looking bad during oral quizzes. Questions were written and displayed, and the teacher went from student to student to obtain the answers. Martin quickly calculated which question would be his, and if he didn't know it he held his handkerchief to his nose and asked to be excused. "I have a nose bleed," he said. Those who knew him snickered at his pretense.

During his high school years, Martin concluded that he should drop out of school and go to work. For at least a semester he worked for an aunt and uncle, but getting up at 4:30 a.m. to begin chores appealed to him less than the boredom of classes. So, heeding his parents' urgings, he returned to school. In later years, he was to enjoy farming as a hobby.

In his high school days Martin was as husky as a young bull: stocky, thick-necked, muscular legs and arms, and shoulders that let you know he was a football player. He was a 180-pound combination of power and speed. His high school team was coached by a Zeeland young man from Hope College who was somewhat older: a brainy fellow named Paul De Kruif, who was later to write such books as *Microbe Hunters* and *Hunger Fighters*. But according to D. J. De Pree, who played football with them, "We couldn't get Martin to keep in training as he should and play regularly." The climax of his last year, 1908, in high school athletics, was a post-season game with one of the two city high schools of Grand Rapids. Their star player that day was a year later named center on the Michigan All-State High School team. The big city team was held scoreless while Martin continually plowed through their line, scoring the only two touchdowns of the afternoon. It must be said that he practically single-handedly won the game for the Zeeland High School against a very formidable team.

In these years Martin apparently showed little indication of what he might do as his life work. If Johanna and Reitze DeHaan hoped he would become a minister, they had little on which to base their hopes, other than faith that God would someday call him.

Three men in the community, besides Uncle Martin, undoubtedly sowed seeds in his mind and heart that would at a later time influence him. One was a veterinarian with whom he enjoyed riding and talking as the vet made calls on his animal patients. Another was Dr. Huizenga, a Zeeland physician. There is no record of how much contact Martin had with the doctor, but he visited the Huizenga home occasionally.

Undoubtedly, he talked more with the doctor's son,

George, a talented fellow who began writing stories for *The American Boy* magazine when he was still in school. A would-be minister who in 1911 dropped out of seminary because of an eye affliction, George had become sort of a heretic by Reformed standards. In seminary George had been assigned to write a paper against premillennialism, but his research work had convinced him that indeed the return of Christ would be premillennial. This affected his own life to the extent that he became a fervent Christian, doing personal work on the streets of Zeeland and sharing Christ over fences to neighbors. George Huizenga told Martin things that he never forgot, things that were in later years to become especially meaningful to him, adding to what he learned from Uncle Martin.

One day a slick character came to town and set up in a hotel, hoping to make a few bucks off curious farmers and gawking schoolboys. A sign he displayed provoked interest: "How smart are you? What is your main talent? What does the future hold for you?" The world-renowned Doctor X. Y. Smartz (or some such name), according to the sign, could "tell all" by a simple reading of one's head.

Martin and Dirk De Pree gazed with awe at the sign and couldn't resist the temptation. Soon with great ceremony the phrenologist was deftly feeling the conformation of the skull of one lad and then the other. To Martin he pronounced, "Someday, my boy, you will be a great public speaker! I predict great things for you. You will be eloquent, and many people will listen to you."

Later, the boys decided they would put the phrenologist to the supreme test. Returning to their homes, they changed into entirely different clothing, then again visited the skull reader.

Would his predictions be the same? To Martin's amazement, the phrenologist uttered the same pronouncement. He was to be a public speaker.

But Mart shrugged it off as a lot of foolishness. "Me? I'm going to be a doctor," he told Dirk De Pree.

Martin DeHaan is the baby
with his brothers and parents

Martin DeHaan's high school days. He is third from left

Two photos of DeHaan in high school.
Upper left is his graduation picture

2 Behold, thou art fair, my love; behold, thou art fair. Thou hast doves' eyes within thy locks; thy hair is as a flock of goats, that appear from Mount Gilead. *Song of Solomon 4:1*

Textbooks and a Blue-Eyed Dutch Girl

It was 1909 — the year that 300-pound President William Howard Taft called a special session of Congress for passage of the Payne Bill, reducing high tariffs; the year that a young bull named Bill Borden, Chicago heir to millions, graduated from Yale intending to go to China as a missionary to the Muslims; and the year that strapping Martin DeHaan, the boy with "oratory bumps" on his head, finished Zeeland High School and contemplated his next step in life. His high brush cut, manly, serious physiognomy, and sturdy, handsome physique made him look several birthdays older than his 18 years. His blue eyes and well-shaped, determined mouth, inherited from his mother, seemed to indicate

31

a desire to succeed in life. Whereas the itinerant phrenologist had predicted Martin would use his mouth to cast spells upon the masses, Martin, as he had told his friend Dirk De Pree, intended to practice medicine and talk on a one-to-one basis, doctor to patient.

While this news probably surprised and pleased Martin's parents, they had to borrow to send him to college — just as they had planned to do for John.

After a year at Hope College in nearby Holland, Martin in October, 1910, boarded the steamer that plied Lake Michigan between Holland and Chicago. In his pocket was an acceptance letter from the College of Medicine of the University of Illinois.

This was Martin's first look at Chicago, and his farthest journey from home. In those days a Zeelander considered even a trip to Grand Rapids or Holland something to talk about, and therefore crossing Lake Michigan to Chicago was the next thing to a voyage to the other side of the world. Chicago must have awed the young Zeelander, with its tall buildings, clattering elevated trains, bustling activity, swarming, seething humanity of all races and colors, and last, and most terrifying to a small-town teenager, its reputation for evil. In some areas of the sprawling lusty metropolis, evil men lurked in the shadows, waiting to step out and mug a passer-by for the change he carried in his pockets. Booze flowed freely, available in taverns and beer gardens in nearly every block. Tawdry women walked certain streets beckoning and smiling foolishly to men with fat wallets. Shootings were numerous and slick, ruthless hoodlums fought the police and each other as they sought wealth to prove that, contrary to the axiom, crime brings rich rewards — for a time.

Chicago was a symphony of fall colors, and there was the smell of burning leaves on the near West Side as Martin began his medical studies.

In those years the College of Medicine was housed principally in an imposing five-story, 200-foot long brick and stone building at the corner of West Harrison and Honore Streets, opposite Cook County Hospital. Among the features were three lecture rooms with a seating capacity of 200 each, a clinical amphitheater seating 300, and an assembly hall for up to 700. It also contained laboratories for physiology, chemistry, materia medica, therapeutics, and microscopical and chemical diagnosis, each capable of accommodating from 50 to 100 students. A three-story annex building contained other laboratories and according to a catalog of that day, "a supply of microscopes, lenses, oil immersions, and a projection apparatus for the illustration of lectures by means of stereopticon views."

The tough program of instruction at this school was "designed to teach the scientific method, to promote learning by problem-solving, and to develop the skills and attitudes of a mature physician." For a boy with only one year of college, it meant hard study.

Fortunately Martin had a photographic mind, able to read a page quickly and recall in detail its contents. His medical books, if stacked on top of each other, likely would have reached the high ceiling of the school library. But he enjoyed the adventure into which each book introduced him. He breezed through material detailing medicine of ancient Egypt, looked in on Greek medicine and Hippocratic physicians, and studied the medieval awakening and the rebirth of science from about 1500-1700. He met a famous artist, Leonardo da Vinci, known for such works as "The Last Supper" and "Mona Lisa." Leonardo, Martin's medical books revealed, had carried out anatomical dissection for many years and later had worked on the preparation of a textbook of anatomy and physiology in collaboration with a young medical teacher.

Martin's mind whirled with a host of other names of men on whose assiduous work modern medicine had been built: such names as Fracastoro, who in 1546 introduced the first rational theory of the nature of infection; Sanctorius, who over a period of some 30 years in the sixteenth and seven-

33

teenth centuries often ate and slept in a balance-chair to lay the foundation of the modern study of metabolism; Lord Lister, who in the 1800's discovered and developed the antiseptic system and made many other important contributions to surgical methods; and William Einthoven, who in 1903 introduced the electrocardiograph.

Often the young medical student from Zeeland studied into the early hours of the morning, memorizing endless lists of details relating to anatomy, biochemistry, physiology, histology, pathology, pharmacology, and many other subjects. Since University of Illinois medical students of those days did not go through internship, he probably had more clinical work than modern-day students do, getting practical experience along with classroom instruction.

By no means did Martin neglect his church life during his medical school years. His mother, worried about her son in wicked Chicago, wrote Dr. John Van Peursem, pastor of a Reformed church in the area, and he took Martin under his wing, encouraging, challenging, advising him. He joined the church, sang in the choir, lending his strong bass to cantatas in which choir members wore Dutch costumes.

During his three years in Chicago, Martin had one especially enjoyable chore after he closed his medical books for the night: writing about thrice weekly to pretty Priscilla Venhuizen.

He had met her during his year at Hope College when he was 19 and she 16 at a wedding in Holland. Priscilla, a blue-eyed brunette who wore her hair in an upsweep was full of life. Somehow she didn't look exactly Holland. Her bachelor uncle, Peter Venhuizen, who lived in her home, said it was "something about her eyes" — they were pretty but not Dutch.

Martin escorted Priscilla home following the wedding festivities and "things progressed nicely after that," as Mrs. DeHaan remembers it today. When he was home in Zeeland, he pedaled a bicycle or rode the interurban train, sort of a Toonerville trolley, to call on her. Dates consisted mainly of buggy rides.

In many respects, Martin's and Priscilla's backgrounds were similar, resting solidly on Reformed theology and tradition. A devout, ramrod-straight man with a moustache and goatee, her father, William Venhuizen, went to church whenever the doors opened, and made the Bible the center of the home.

While in Chicago the first fall, Martin was already saving money to buy an engagement ring for Priscilla. To help do so he skipped breakfast and skimped on lunch, subsisting on soup to which he added water and an extra amount of crackers. His no-breakfast plan became a habit that lasted for years, but once he had purchased the ring he began eating normal lunches.

Home for Christmas, Martin shoved medicine far from his thoughts and headed for Priscilla's. She had invited him for dinner, but he couldn't wait and arrived early to present her with the ring he had sacrificed to buy — a modest diamond in a yellow gold tiffany setting.

Priscilla and Martin began to lay plans for their wedding on June 25, 1914, following his graduation on June 11.

Meantime, Martin busied himself preparing for the day he would go into medical practice. On May 21 he made a trip to Lansing, the state capital, to appear before the state medical board. Though he must have faced this august body with some fear and apprehension, he received an average rating of 90.4% on the following subjects: anatomy, physiology, chemistry, pathology, materia medica, therapeutics, toxicology, histology, practice of medicine, surgery, obstetrics, mental and nervous diseases, diseases of the eye, ear, nose, and throat, bacteriology, hygiene, and public health laws of Michigan. His certificate was dated June 24, the day before the wedding.

Priscilla made the trip by steamer across Lake Michigan to attend Martin's graduation. There was probably no prouder person in the Studebaker Theater that morning of

June 11 for the 32nd annual commencement of the University of Illinois College of Medicine than Priscilla Venhuizen. For following the conferring of degrees by Dr. Edmund Janes James, president of the university, the valedictory was delivered by Martin Ralph DeHaan, M.D. At 23, he was the youngest of his class of 111. Unfortunately, there is no record of the young doctor's oration.

Two weeks later, on Thursday, June 25, the day dawned bright and warm in Holland. Martin arose relatively early in Zeeland, undoubtedly a little more nervous than he had been two weeks earlier when he had delivered his valedictory. In her home on the outskirts of Holland, Priscilla excitedly directed the last-minute affairs for the wedding, which was to be held in her front yard. Members of the family picked daisies from along the railroad tracks and shortly before time for the ceremony erected a lattice of ferns and daisies beneath a large maple tree.

Here, at 6 p.m. young Doctor DeHaan and Priscilla Venhuizen, dressed in her white gown with a long train, stood before Dr. John Van Peursem, Martin's Chicago pastor who had come to take a church in the area. Two little flower girls stood by, and William Venhuizen gave Priscilla away. A soft breeze rustled the leaves on the maple tree, and the Venhuizen cow grazed peacefully nearby as at 6:15 Dr. Van Peursem uttered the meaningful words: "And now, by the authority vested in me as a minister of the Gospel and the laws of the state of Michigan, I do solemnly pronounce you to be — husband and wife."

Following the wedding dinner Dr. and Mrs. M. R. DeHaan rode the interurban to Muskegon, 34 miles away, where they spent several days honeymooning at the home of Benjamin Oosterbaan, a cousin of Martin's. Among other activities, they did a bit of boating, recalls Mrs. DeHaan. And they were pestered a bit by the Oosterbaans' eight-year-old son, Bennie, who was to become the only three-time All-American

36

football player at the University of Michigan and who was to coach the Wolverines from 1948-1958.

In a real sense, the honeymoon was to last for 51 years, until Martin's death, but following the visit to Muskegon the newlyweds came back to Holland to face reality.

"All we had was debt when we married — we were so poor we couldn't even afford to have pictures taken," Mrs. DeHaan chuckles, remembering those early days. "Martin had every intention of repaying his father for sending him through medical school, and ultimately he did so."

At this point Martin had no idea where he would practice. He wanted to stay in the area. And above all he wanted to live up to his class motto: *"Prodesse Quam Conspiceri"* (to be of service rather than to be in the limelight).

DeHaan on his graduation day from the University of Illinois
Medical School, 1914

At the University of Illinois Medical School, June 11, 1914

3

To every thing there is a season . . . a time to be born, and a time to die; . . . and a time to heal. . . . *Ecclesiastes 3:1-3*

Country Doctor

In late summer of 1914, newsboys at corners of big cities had plenty to shout about. In the world of sports Jim Thorpe, the Sac and Fox Indian who was perhaps the greatest all-around athlete in U. S. sports annals, was in his heyday. Fireballer Walter Johnson, who had won 36 games for Washington in 1913, was hard at it again. Babe Ruth, remembered today for his home runs, made his debut with the Boston Red Sox as an ace pitcher. Jack Dempsey was emerging as the big name in boxing, and Barney Oldfield was a household name among auto racing fans. In more serious news, President Woodrow Wilson and his Secretary of State, William Jennings Bryan, began a parting of the ways as they discussed the role of the U.S. in relation to a general European war that had ignited from a squabble between Austria and Serbia, crowding Wilson's domestic issues off front pages of American newspapers. This of course, was the beginning of World War I.

But in the little country town of Byron Center, Michigan, 14 miles due east of Zeeland, the big news was that young Martin DeHaan, M.D., was coming to hang out his shingle. Townspeople and farmers in the surrounding area had become disillusioned with one doctor, and the town's other M.D. couldn't handle everyone.

Actually, a letter to Martin's parents from an unhappy patient in Byron Center brought "Doc," as he was becoming known to his friends and family, to the little farming community. In a borrowed horse and buggy he and Priscilla drove out to investigate. He had already looked into one or two other practice opportunities in the general area, but when he visited Byron Center and talked with the people he was soon convinced that this was his town.

The day Doc arrived with a wagonload of equipment and furniture, a patient was waiting on the front porch of the big two-story faded-red house on Main Street that he had rented. And others were coming in the next days before he and Priscilla could put the house in order.

The parlor served as Doc's office, and the living room as the waiting room; when it overflowed, patients sat on the stairway to the second floor. Among other things, the office contained a sterilizer heated by an alcohol flame, an examining table, and a medicine box from which Doc dispensed his own medicines.

The house was heated by three potbellied stoves, and with no electricity, the DeHaans used old-fashioned kerosene lamps to light the office and other rooms.

Doc added to their debt when he borrowed to buy a horse and buggy, and a cutter to be used in winter. Later, he added a Model T Ford to his means of transportation, but it could be used only when the rutty, narrow roads were dry — and this was mainly in summer and early fall.

In time he was able to pay his debts, including the money he owed his father for schooling. Actually, the money came surprisingly rapidly, though in his first year or so charges for his medical work were ridiculously low when compared to modern-day rates: 50¢ for an office call, 50¢ or 75¢ for a house call, and $7.50 for an obstetrics case.

Within the first year of his practice, young Doctor DeHaan, wearing a moustache for a more mature look, was treating patients from a wide area of the flat farm country. In making house calls, he quickly learned every shortcut. Hour after hour, day after day, through rain, sleet, and snow, and summer drought, he drove his Ford, buggy, or cutter to bring medical help and comfort to residents of the area.

A spring day might find him driving his creaking, mud-splattered black buggy through a driving March rain six miles to reach patients as far north of Byron Center as Grandville, Wyoming and southwest Grand Rapids; the next day the ringing of the long-necked wall phone might send him about ten miles west to Vriesland, five miles east into the Cutlerville area, or about eight miles south to Dorr. Rarely, however, did he go out for single calls. Usually he made several, and on certain days he saw patients at a designated place, usually a home graciously opened up for the purpose.

More than once in an emergency someone rushed Doc to a patient by handcar on the interurban railroad tracks.

These were adventurous but body-wearing days, and Doc often, after being out late the night before on calls, wasn't ready for his early morning patients. Usually they came into town with milk for the creamery, and farm wagons began stopping out front of Doc DeHaan's before 7 a.m. Mrs. DeHaan, always an early riser, greeted patients and assured them that the Doctor would be ready to see them shortly. Sometimes she had to stir him the second time before he rolled out, splashed cold water on his face, and dressed.

Fortified with a cup of strong, black, steaming coffee, he was soon bursting with energy and drawing wisely on his vast medical knowledge and common sense to try to stop disease and pain. Though rather brusque in his manner and with a rough exterior, he handled patients gently, talking to them at length and listening to their problems. He did all within his means to meet their needs.

"He must have become intensely involved with people, to the point that it became terribly frustrating, and the lack of modern medications to help matters added greatly to the problem," muses Dr. DeHaan's son, Marvin, himself a highly successful physician turned psychiatrist who practices in Wheaton, Illinois.

"Among the basic medications which we have today, he would have had only three — aspirin, morphine, and digitalis."

For all practical purposes, the era of modern medicine was still in its early stages. Yet great advances were being made. For example, in 1911 Alexis Carrel was awarded the Nobel Prize for his work on vascular suture and the transplantation of blood vessels and organs; and Charles Richet had been so honored in 1913 in recognition of his work on anaphylaxis; and Robert Barany received the award in 1914 for his work on the physiology and pathology of the vestibular apparatus. But there were inept medications being used by doctors everywhere.

Horse-and-buggy doctors, as well as big-city physicians, prescribed both good and questionable vegetable drugs, among them, asafetida, cajuput, cannabis indica, camomile, croton oil, creosote, clove, mustard, spearmint, squill, and valerian, all of which have long gone out of style for one reason or another. How many of these Dr. DeHaan dispensed to his patients the records do not tell. But what he did use he believed in and when he prescribed remedies for his patients, he fully expected them to follow directions. He was a great believer in mustard plasters for respiratory ailments, contemporaries remember, and magnesium sulphate (Epsom salts) was his standard remedy for several ailments, helpful especially for relieving the system of excess fluids.

It was Epsom salts prescribed by Doc that presumably saved the life of his sister Ada. She recalls:

"I had diphtheria and was very sick. I was 21 at the time and still living in Zeeland. Our doctor gave me a shot but it didn't help. I got worse and the folks wanted Mart to see me. But we didn't have telephone service during the day, so they had to wait till after 6 o'clock to call him. He got there about 9 o'clock and gave me Epsom salts and that did the trick. It relieved the water that was backing up in my kidneys. The medicine the Zeeland doctor had given me was good, but he hadn't given me enough, and it was too slow acting."

Epsom salts also saved the day — and a lot of painful scratching — for Maynard Vander Zaag, a neighbor youth who drove regularly for Doc from late fall to spring for several years. Now a retired electrical inspector and living in Grand Rapids, he chuckles as he remembers the incident:

"One time the itch was going around, and I got it on my thigh and began scratching till it bled. Doc was making up a sulfur salve and putting it in jars for patients with this annoying itch. 'Here, put this on,' he'd say, 'and leave your underwear on till the itch is gone. But put the salve on every day.'

"Well," Vander Zaag chuckles, "a guy's underwear would get stiff as a board, till it could stand on end, and I didn't want any of that. So I told Doc I wanted something else. 'Look, Doc, I can't sleep nights, but give me something else besides that sulfur salve,' I said. Well, he told me to go home and dissolve as much Epsom salts in hot water as I could and to sponge the affected area. 'That'll take care of it,' Doc promised.

"Well, I followed his directions, and I bet I dissolved at least a pound of Epsom salts in hot water. I took my sponge bath, and paced the floor for about 15 minutes till the sting went away. The next morning my brother asked, 'How did you sleep last night?' 'Like a baby,' I said. Then I told him about the Epsom salts, and he decided to try it, for he had the itch too. Well, he tried it and I heard him hollering in there (boy! did that stuff sting!). But it cured him. After that he slept too."

An episode of a more serious nature involving his youthful driver features Dr. DeHaan in the role of surgeon and illustrates the conditions under which he sometimes operated. It all started the evening Maynard's mother called Doc over to see the youth, who had severe pains about the abdomen.

"Minnerd," Doc said after examining him — it was never Maynard with Doc, always *Minnerd* — "it could be appendicitis. I don't know for sure, but we're going to keep an eye on this thing."

Doc called for standard treatment of that period, prescribing hot bags of salt to be applied to the abdomen throughout the night. Then, after examining Maynard next morning, he ordered a switch to ice packs, apparently hoping to reduce the inflammation if it was appendicitis, or stop the muscle spasm if that was the problem. This seemed to remedy the ailment, as the pain subsided. But a few days later Maynard complained of pain again, and Doc announced that an appendectomy was imperative.

But Maynard's mother balked. Operations were dangerous. She didn't want her son going off to the hospital in Grand Rapids. If it had to be done, couldn't it be done at home? Doc said it could, though he preferred to do it in the hospital. Finally Doc agreed to operate in the home, with the assistance of a Grand Rapids surgeon. But still Maynard's mother hesitated.

Doc turned to the boy. "Minnerd, do you want an operation or not? We'll let you decide."

Maynard allowed that he'd "never be any good this way anyhow — may as well take 'er out, Doc."

The physician turned to Mrs. Vander Zaag. "Tonight at 8 o'clock we'll be here."

46

"Bring me a pretty nurse," the perky patient joshed.

"You leave the nurse to me," Doc said, a twinkle in his eye, and disappeared out the door.

The nurse he brought that night wasn't exactly what Maynard had in mind, but "she was a fine nurse," Vander Zaag remembers. Dr. DeHaan also brought Dr. Lyman along and they rigged up lights after getting a battery from the garage. The nurse scrubbed the dining room table antiseptic clean. Maynard stretched out on the table, ether was administered, and the operation was underway.

After the appendix was out and the patient in bed, Doc gave orders that the boy needed rest for ten days. "I'll keep an eye on him — he's my driver and we've got to take good care of him and get him back on his feet."

Interestingly, Dr. DeHaan lacked the long, thin hands generally associated with a surgeon. His hands were rather chubby with stubby fingers, but he used them expertly — just as he did in later years as a fly fisherman: "He was an expert at tying a fly onto the line — just a few movements and he had it done quick as a wink," comments a fishing companion.

In connection with his surgery, most was done in Grand Rapids in the hospital. "It was the minor, traumatic type, such as a farm worker cutting off a finger, that he did in the home or in his office," his son Marvin recalls from conversations with his father. "When he was required to operate in a home, he used relatives and friends to help. He carried all the necessary instruments and other items with him — scalpel, hemostats, needles, sutures, gauze — and was prepared for an emergency. He used thread for suture material, boiling it.

"He did tonsillectomies, generally in his office. I'm still amazed at how tonsils were taken out, and how they got away with it without hemorrhaging," says Marvin. "I think he had a loop of wire and it went around the tonsil; a pull on the wire snipped it off. They put a pack in to stop the bleeding. In the light of present-day practice, it must have taken quite a lot of nerve to do things that way."

Probably nothing brought as much delight to the Doctor's life as ushering new lives into the world — and there are many still living in the Byron Center area who received their first spanking from the hand of Dr. DeHaan. But these adventures in obstetrics cost him many sleepless nights and other hardships. For example, at times he battled howling storms to reach women in labor. The winter of 1914-15 was probably the worst. In some of the storms steam and electric railway traffic in nearby Grand Rapids was all but paralyzed. On January 28, 1915, even the moderating effects of Lake Michigan failed to keep the mercury from dipping below zero. But icy winds, zero temperatures and snow didn't stall the country doctor, for babies wouldn't wait. Dressed in his bearskin coat and fur cap, a horsehide blanket over his lap and a heated soapstone or lighted lantern at his feet, undaunted, he hit the roads day or night in a cutter pulled over the hoary roads by a faithful horse.

Once, on a frosty night, Maynard Vander Zaag drove the Doctor in the sputtering Model T to a farm home where a German woman was in labor. Usually in such situations, Maynard remained outside, but after a few minutes Doctor opened the door and called, "Minnerd, it's probably going to be a long wait. Better drain the water out of the radiator and bring some blankets in and get some rest on the kitchen floor."

Vander Zaag tells the rest:

"I tried to sleep but I couldn't. I heard this woman taking on, and her husband was in the kitchen with me, beside himself, pacing the floor. Then all at once we heard a baby cry, and his face brightened. With a German accent, he bellowed in relief, 'I'm glad that's over with!' Then pretty soon he heard another one cry, too. Then he moaned, 'My goodness, that's seven kids in six years!' Now he began pacing the floor not knowing what to do, for he was quite poor."

Vander Zaag recalls this fact: "I've got to give Doc credit

48

— if they were poor people he'd do a case like that for almost nothing. He'd cut the $7.50 price way down. He was really good-hearted."

Sometimes people paid the doctor in farm products. On one occasion, after he cared for a farmer who had broken his leg, he learned the man was going to sell his cow to pay the bill. But Doc turned thumbs down — and told him to consider his account paid — the cow was the man's only source of milk and butter for his family.

Dr. DeHaan delighted in meeting patients — and his "children" that he delivered — in later years. He enjoyed telling about the twins "born a year apart," as he termed it. He was reminded of the incident 48 years later as he was shopping in a hardware store when a man shook his hand and began, "You are Dr. DeHaan, I believe. You attended my first 'birthday party'; in fact, you were the master of ceremonies." Then he went on to remind Doctor that he had attended his mother when he and his twin brother were born — one at 11:50 p.m., December 31, 1916, and the other on January 1, 1917, at 12:15 a.m.

"Yes, indeed, I remember!" exclaimed Dr. DeHaan. "It was quite a noisy New Year's party, especially after I gave the two of you your first spankings."

But what thrilled Dr. DeHaan even more than being reminded of the incident was the news that the twin brothers had had another birthday — on the same night 18 years later. Both had been born again of the Spirit of God in a gospel meeting.

Dr. Marvin DeHaan, again recalling medical shoptalk with his father, reminds that there were occasionally frustrating, disappointing experiences connected with OB cases. "For him OB was either a lot of fun or tragic. It can be an easy procedure, but on the other hand if he were to get into a massive hemorrhage he had two lives at stake within a very few minutes. It goes from one extreme to the other. Here he would have parents who have been expecting this new life for nine months, and then suddenly there's a problem.

I know he had some tragic situations where both the child and mother died. It can be a most traumatic experience, because it's so opposed to what the family was expecting would happen."

Marvin DeHaan continues: "I think sometimes he used medication to help labor along — probably castor oil or quinine. While he was forced to sit through many a night when possibly the baby had turned, it was sometimes desirable, under certain conditions, to speed up the process.

"The delivery would be right there in the bed, on a rubber pad or sheet that he carried with him. Occasionally he used forceps, but this was not common. The night deliveries, at least in his earlier years of practice, were done by the light of kerosene lamps, and generally he worked without assistance, except a helping hand from a family member."

Naturally, despite his rugged constitution, Doc DeHaan sometimes felt almost drained of strength and much in need of rest, following a protracted vigil at the bedside of an expectant mother, or after a long day of house calls. On occasion, he got some sleep in a home, or, on calls, in the back seat of the Model T as Maynard drove along. Often on routine calling days, he didn't get home till nearly midnight, and there were times he returned home on a Sunday morning in time to nod a greeting to folk on their way to church.

Once he was so weary he fell asleep while driving the cutter, and the outcome could have been tragic. Dr. DeHaan described the incident in these words:*

"It was in the early hours of a February morning when I was coming home in my cutter. The weather was bitter cold and my legs were wrapped in a heavy robe, with a lighted kerosene lantern between my feet. I pulled the collar of my bearskin coat around my head and fell fast asleep. Toots, a small bay mare who knew the way home, plodded on. Suddenly I awoke to hear the roar of a locomotive! I sat

*Our Daily Bread, March 19, 1963.

up — and, lo, Toots had heard the train coming and had stopped about 25 feet from the track."

It was well known that Doctor loved his horses — and especially gentle, intelligent Toots. But he even had affection for Boob, "a big, black, one-eyed brute who was the dumbest creature I ever knew." Undoubtedly his favorite was Billy, the first horse he owned — the friskiest of several that worked for the doctor, and Doc vowed he'd never sell him. "I'll keep Billy as long as he lives," he once told Maynard. And he did. Billy was the type of horse that couldn't be stopped, giving a second effort when the cutter hit a dry spot in the road, pulling it across with seemingly little effort. The more Doc drove Billy the wilder he got. One day, to Doc's sorrow, Billy made his last house call with his owner, dropping dead on the road. A painting of the majestic, chestnut Billy hangs today in Dr. DeHaan's study at his home.

In many respects, the country doctor himself was a man with the nature of Billy — full of zest, forging ahead against obstacles that would stop most men, and, yes, even a bit frisky at times. People in the area were glad he had chosen Byron Center — and they were to be especially grateful for such a doctor during the difficult, terrifying days of the flu pandemic of 1918-19.

Dr. and Mrs. DeHaan and Ruth

The first house in Byron Center (at right)
and Dr. DeHaan with his favorite horse, "Billy"

econd house in Byron Center

4

And there was a great cry in Egypt. . . . *Exodus 12:30*

The Pandemic

A biting west wind of up to 25 mph, picking up moisture from Lake Michigan, dumped 15 inches of snow on the Byron Center area in mid-January 1918, adding to seven inches already on the ground. Then the mercury dipped to 14 degrees below zero. Country roads were blocked with snowdrifts for days. Typically, 26-year-old Dr. Martin Ralph DeHaan, deferred from duty in World War I because he was needed on the homefront, made calls just the same, riding his cutter as far as he could go to reach a home, then blanketing down his horse and hiking the rest of the way on foot.

The worst foe of his medical career was yet to come — and it wasn't to be weather. It started innocently enough in June. He examined a patient who complained of a headache, fever, and prostration.

"You've got a case of old-fashioned flu. Aspirin, plenty of liquids, and rest. You should be all right in a few days."

But unknown then to Byron Center's busy doctor, thousands of other doctors in Michigan, across the United States, and around the world were encountering similar conditions.

The first wave of the notorious influenza pandemic hit in June and July; cases were numerous but few died from the disease. Then came a second wave in October and November. Millions around the world fell victim to a more potent form of influenza. After contracting the malady, about one fifth of the patients died — within hours in many instances. In February, 1919, a third wave swept the world, and the disease this time was fatal especially to youths and young adults.

In the U.S. alone during the prolonged pandemic, an estimated 20 million persons contracted the disease and some 450,000 died. The mortality rate rose to the fantastic level of 584.5 per 100,000 population, almost 3.5 times the 1917 figure. The influenza pandemic was also associated with the rise of mortality from other respiratory diseases such as whooping cough and tuberculosis.

Among his writings, Dr. DeHaan left this brief account[*] of the pandemic in the area he served:

"People fell like sticks before a tornado. In some families eight, nine or ten were sick at the same time. Some also had pneumonia. Outside the temperature hovered around zero. From everywhere the calls for help came, and we were unable to reach many for several days. For five days and nights at a time I never took off my clothes, but snatched a bit of sleep in the car while being driven, or on a couch while waiting for a baby to be born of a mother with a fever of 105 degrees."

During these days he lived almost exclusively on raw eggs and milk.

[*]*Our Daily Bread,* September 14, 1959.

Maynard Vander Zaag, the driver who served the doctor for several years, recalls that he put in the longest day of his life with the doctor during the second wave of the pandemic. They worked from 5 a.m. one day till 5 o'clock the next morning. They began the day by driving the Ford to North Dorr, south of Byron Center, to pick up a young woman with appendicitis. After taking her to a hospital in Grand Rapids, Dr. DeHaan assisted another surgeon in the operation. Then Maynard drove him back to the Byron Center area, and Doctor made some 40 to 50 calls in homes to treat flu victims.

One of Doc's remedies in treating flu cases was the mustard plaster, used when victims developed respiratory problems. A paste mixture of powdered mustard, flour, and water sandwiched in a cloth, it worked well only on thin people DeHaan believed. On a call to North Dorr, he examined an obese young woman, a victim of flu. He prescribed medication but lamented to her father that he doubted his best remedy — a mustard plaster — would help her, for she was too fat for it to penetrate. On Doctor's next call, his driver saw gloom over the physician's countenance as he emerged. His patient had died.

"He was one of the best flu doctors in the whole area," commented a contemporary. "He lost fewer patients than any doctor that I know of. He seemed to have the right idea with that mustard plaster. I know. When I'd get a cold that I couldn't break, I'd get a mustard plaster and that usually fixed me up."

It was March 25, 1919, during the flu epidemic that the DeHaans' second child, June, was born. Ruth, the first, was born June 1, 1916, and, as in the case of all four DeHaan children — two boys were to follow — their attending obstetrician was Dr. M. R. DeHaan. Another physician attended Priscilla during her pregnancies, but her husband performed the deliveries.

There was nothing DeHaan enjoyed more than his medical

work itself. He was in his element while diagnosing and treating patients. When the crank of a Model T kicked back, breaking the owner's arm, the Doctor delighted in being of service. Once he was called to save the lives of an entire family when a mother inadvertently added lead arsenate to her pancake batter. He felt a purpose was being fulfilled in his life as he answered emergency calls.

Probably one of the most rewarding things Dr. DeHaan did was in connection with his mother. While she was visiting him once in Byron Center, Martin looked at her and asked, "Were you crying? Your eyes are red." He examined her carefully and concluded that diabetes had been the problem bothering her for years. Insulin had recently been discovered, and he put her on it, giving her a new lease on life.

As far as Martin R. DeHaan, M.D., knew he would be a country doctor all his days. He and Priscilla had bought a home in 1919, better suited to a doctor's practice than the house on Main Street. Among other more modern facilities, it had battery powered electricity and a furnace. But a series of events began that was to change the course of his life drastically.

In October, 1921, Dr. DeHaan experienced an unusual toothache. At first it seemed to be a problem for a local dentist, but his condition worsened and he was hospitalized in Grand Rapids. The tooth was extracted and he was given an injection containing horse serum. Within a day after he had returned home, his system had reacted violently to it. Hives covered his body; his eyes were swollen shut. Priscilla bathed him with soda water.

Suffering much pain and discomfort, he was eventually readmitted to the hospital, in critical condition. He was destined to live, however, though the Martin Ralph DeHaan who was to return to Byron Center a few days later was to be a different person — one with the same rugged exterior, but a man with new goals, new attitudes, a new life within. During his years as a physician, he had acquired a rather stout appetite for alcohol, some of his patients having given him wine, hard cider, and liquors to show their hospitality when he made house calls. The Lord was to deal with him concerning this, as well as other fleshly habits.

The wonderful transformation to be wrought by the Son of God in his life was, however, to bring sorrow to the people of the Byron Center area. For because of it the beloved physician would terminate his practice and, under God's leading, begin a new career that would ultimately find him doctoring spiritual ills of people around the world.

5   Therefore, if any man be in Christ, he is a new
     creation. . . . *2 Corinthians 5:17*

A New Man

It it well known that some people, facing death, see their
past deeds flash before them. There's no written record of
what transpired in the mind of 30-year-old Martin Ralph
DeHaan, M.D., as he struggled for life in October, 1921, in a
Grand Rapids hospital. But it is known he did considerable
thinking about his past — and about his future.

For all of his 30 years he had been identified with the
church. As a boy he had gone regularly, and even in medical
school he had been faithful in attendance. In Byron Center
he and Priscilla had joined the Byron Center Reformed
Church, and he had attended when he could. But his life
hadn't been counting for God as it should have. There were

sins in his life, at which God's finger was pointing. He felt condemned, though as a 12-year-old boy he had presumably settled his relationship with God.

Nurses passed silently in the hallway outside his room as a quiet transaction took place in the heart and life of the patient from Byron Center. Again, there's no record of the conversation he had with God. He never made a point of telling and retelling the experience. But in 1929 he penned these words: "I was born in 1891 of the flesh, 'a child of wrath even as others.' After a life of sin for 31 years I was born again of the Spirit in October, 1922.* Since then my only hope and aim is to exalt Him to whom be all glory forever and ever. Eph. 1:7."

Priscilla, who learned of his spiritual experience when she visited him in the hospital shortly after it happened, recalls that as he talked about it afterward he mentioned that he wasn't sure he had truly met God at age 12. The hospital experience was a spiritual struggle not unlike Jacob's, who wrestled with God, as it were, until dawn before he received a new touch and blessing from the divine hand. "Spare my life and I'll serve You," Dr. DeHaan pleaded with God. And evidently he meant it with all his heart, for, after he went home a few days later and soon resumed his practice, God rode with him in his buggy or car. And there were quiet conversations about the future — about how the doctor would fulfill his pledge of service.

Neighbors noticed the difference. The DeHaans were among the few families who owned a phonograph, and, according to a longtime resident of Byron Center, "When their windows were open we could hear such songs as 'Since Jesus Came Into My Heart.' "

Farmers in their fields, and children at play, and even his horses, must have wondered what had happened to Doc, for

*From all indications, Dr. DeHaan's memory played a trick on him. He was in seminary in the fall of 1922 and living in Holland, according to records of Western Theological Seminary and the American Medical Association. Thus he was 30 when his conversion occurred in October, 1921.

from time to time Mrs. DeHaan accompanied him on house calls and they enjoyed singing glad songs of the faith as they rode along like a honeymooning couple in the buggy. "He had such joy in his heart that he liked to sing about it," recalls Mrs. DeHaan.

It wasn't only knowledge of sins forgiven that made Doc burst with joy. This was enough, to be sure. But the idea that at 30 he was going to serve God brought great delight to him. He felt that, at last, he was stepping into the shoes of his brother John, who had drowned before seeing his — and his parents' — dream fulfilled of becoming a minister.

And, as might be expected, when Martin told his mother the news, she wept with joy. God had answered her prayers concerning her son's waywardness, and now, at last, He was giving her a minister-son. He was blessing her beyond measure.

M. R. DeHaan gave much credit to his mother for what had happened to him: "I was blessed with a godly, praying mother, and her admonitions have never left me. I can still close my eyes and in memory see her kneeling at her bed, wiping the tears from her eyes with her blue checkered apron. Oh, precious, blessed memories! It was Mother's prayers which influenced me more than all the preaching to which I was exposed with unfailing regularity."

He also wrote with a grateful heart of his father: "His life of prayer, his study of the Word, his faithful habit of teaching his children are memories more precious than I can tell."

As the weeks passed, Doctor talked with Priscilla — and with God — about the kind of Christian service he should do. Preach? Become a missionary? He wasn't sure. He talked about going abroad as a missionary, but friends pointed out that he could continue his practice, be God's man on the job, and at the same time support a missionary. For a time he thought perhaps this was the answer.

The matter continued to burden him increasingly, until finally, one day in early spring of 1922, he came in from house calls and said, "Mother, I can't go on any longer." In an act of finality, he slid his medical bag across the kitchen floor. "This is it!" He then sold his practice, his home and office equipment, and the young doctor made plans to enter Western Theological Seminary, the Reformed Church seminary in nearby Holland.

The transformation that had occurred in his life continued to amaze DeHaan no end. As he read and studied his Bible, he saw it all a matter of God's grace. In later years he was to make a careful study of the grace of God, and pen these words concerning the subject:

"Like electricity, light and life, we know only what it [grace] does, rather than what it is. Why God should choose the meanest, basest, most unworthy individuals with absolutely nothing to commend them at all to God, except their miserable, lost condition, and then exalt them to become the sons of God, members of the divine family, and use them for His glory, is beyond all reason and human understanding. Yet that is grace."

That he saw himself as the object of God's grace is illustrated in an incident that he related:

"Some time ago on my way to Colorado, I stopped off to visit my son, Marvin, on Chicago's North Side. After parking my car I took a shortcut to the apartment, through one of Chicago's North Side alleys, and there amid the dust and the refuse and the filth and rats, I encountered one of the most pathetic sights I have ever beheld.

"There, beside a leaking barrel filled with garbage, and black with flies, stood one of society's outcasts, a man about 65 years old. Only the rim of his tattered hat was left, his shoes were tied on with rope, his coat in shreds, his trousers in tatters, his hands black with filth, his hair matted together, his beard even worse. I watched him as he pawed about in the garbage, pulled out a whisky bottle with a teaspoon of its poison left, and lifted it to his lips. He found another drop or two in another bottle, and then he fished out a crust of garbage-sodden bread and placed it in his mouth with his filthy hands. As I stood there, I . . . said to myself, 'O God, O God! That's me! That's me, apart from Thy wonderful grace.' . . . Under similar circumstances of birth, environment and opportunity, I would have been no different, and no better. What a humbling truth grace is!"

In experiencing God's grace, M. R. DeHaan had been born from above. He found himself not merely a sinner redeemed from Hell and on the way to Heaven, but he began to discover that God had imparted His very own life deep within. Yet, strangely, he was human as ever and still a Hollander through and through; his temperament hadn't changed and he realized he was subject to temptations as before. But his new God-implanted life made a world of difference. He had a ready source of victory: the indwelling Holy Spirit, a mighty Savior and Friend, Jesus Christ, and an omnipotent heavenly Father.

In a real sense 2 Corinthians 5:17 was being worked out in his experience: "Therefore, if any man be in Christ, he is a new creation; old things are passed away; behold, all things are become new."

Perhaps the most marked example of triumph in the Doctor's life came one day shortly before he gave up his practice. A grateful patient proudly presented a gift to the faithful physician. It was a bottle of liquor. DeHaan took the bottle home. All the way the Holy Spirit tugged at his conscience. "You know how strong drink has made a fool of you," He seemed to say. "You've determined to give it up now that you are Christ's. Rely on Me; I'll help you. . . ."

When the Doctor showed the bottle to Priscilla, fear gripped her heart. How she had prayed that he would quit the miserable habit! But praise to God replaced the fear as he resolutely shook his head and said, "I don't dare keep it; it simply would not honor the Lord, Mother." Ceremoniously, he poured the cursed contents of the bottle down the drain. It dramatically signified a mighty victory over a fleshly habit he had come to hate — but which he by himself had been unable to break. God had done it for him. He was free!

But this did not mean that the beloved physician did not have battles with more subtle forms of sin. For example, like a thorn in the flesh, his temperament, marked by occasional outbursts of temper, impetuosity, and what some termed "Dutch stubbornness," continued to keep him keenly aware that he hadn't reached a state of sinless perfection.

Once at a picnic, so the story goes, Doc hit a grounder in a baseball game and the umpire called him out at first base. Certain that he was safe, he argued till the ump and his own teammates turned away and continued the game, ignoring Doc on first. An inning or two later, when the call came for supper, the still simmering DeHaan remained determinedly camped on first.

In regard to his temper, Dr. DeHaan was to mellow considerably over the years, and was to be greatly loved by thousands. But his temperament also kept him on his knees before the Lord.

In 1954, in his book *Simon Peter,* Dr. DeHaan, pointing out that Peter was both a sinner and a saint, showed that the apostle Paul recognized a constant struggle between the evil nature and the new nature. DeHaan cited Paul's statement in Romans 7:20, "Now if I do that I would not, it is no more I that do it, but sin that dwelleth in me." The writer pointed out that "Paul wrote this thirty years after he had been saved, and had become a new creation in Christ. He still realized his danger, he knew his need of help outside of himself, and he made no claim or boast of having gotten rid of the old man, once and for all. Paul realized the hopelessness of battling in his own strength, and turned it all over to the Lord Jesus Christ for victory."

He continued by asserting that, whereas Paul claimed the victory, it did not imply that the flesh had been done away with or eradicated; actually, he said, "the older it becomes the more rotten it seems to be."

In his book *Law or Grace* DeHaan berated those who

consider themselves completely free from the power of sin: "Unfortunately, there are some poor, blind, mistaken people who claim sinless perfection. They tell us the old sinful nature has been eradicated, root and branch, and they never sin any more. To them the Lord Jesus Christ is wasting His time at the right hand of God as our interceding High Priest, for they have nothing to confess, and need no one to intercede for them."

Often DeHaan made reference to his gratefulness to God for including 1 John 2:1 in the Bible: "If any man sin, we have an advocate with the Father, Jesus Christ the righteous."

In the case of M. R. DeHaan, like Peter and Paul, he laid his frailties before the Lord, doggedly served and worshiped Him and was destined to become one of God's spiritual giants. The Lord was to use his keen mind that had won him valedictory honors in medical school and his ready tongue to proclaim the Gospel of Christ to millions from pulpits and through radio. Even his stubbornness and staunch determination were to be harnessed to stand against all forms of spiritual error. To begin with, he was to shake his fist like a Martin Luther in the faces of leaders of his denomination and tell them that he believed they were not following the clear teachings of the Bible.

It would happen in Grand Rapids in his first pastorate, where he would be branded a heretic by some and a heroic defender of the Faith by others.

Graduating class at Western Semir
(DeHaan is at center with bow

6 Preach the word; be diligent in season, out of season; reprove, rebuke, exhort with all long-suffering and doctrine. *2 Timothy 4:2*

Tempest in Grand Rapids

Sometimes in the months after Martin decided to sell his practice in Byron Center and enter seminary, he and Priscilla wrestled with occasional doubts. Were they really doing the right thing? If God wanted him in seminary, then why didn't He find suitable housing for them in Holland, where the seminary was situated? By late spring of 1922 they had spent many hours poring over the classified ads of the Holland newspapers, and knocking at doors, but each trip to Holland brought only disappointment.

Finally, Priscilla and Martin rented a furnished house from seminary students who were to be away for the summer. Among the items that Martin brought from Byron Center was his medical bag and reputation as a capable physician and surgeon. This proved providential, for some of his former patients drove or rode the interurban to Holland to see him, and others nearby also knocked at his door for medical assistance.

A fellow seminary student, the Rev. Edward H. Tanis, recalls: "Following a bout that I had with tonsillitis, Doc recommended removal of my tonsils, and, along with another city physician, took them out right there in his office. DeHaan was a good doctor. Once he was a bit tardy for a class, and as he entered he held up two fingers. He had just delivered twins."

The DeHaans welcomed the income from the out-of-the-bag practice, aware that even with their substantial savings Doctor's three years in seminary would not be an easy matter financially. By this time, of course, Ruth was a sprouting six-year-old, and June was half as old.

After the DeHaans moved into another house and Martin was well into his studies at Western Theological Seminary, the lusty cry of a baby boy told the girls that the scepter had passed from them. The date was February 21, 1923; the obstetrician, seminarian M. R. DeHaan; and the young heir, Richard William.

The proud young father returned to classes, carrying, besides his Scofield Reference Bible and theology books, cherished first impressions of the beet-faced son to whom he had administered his first hard pat on the rump. Likely on his first day back in seminary following Richard's arrival the student-father wasn't fully tuned in on the lectures of such distinguished faculty members as Albertus Pieters, John R. Mulder, E. J. Blekkink, and John E. Kuizenga, the latter of whom spent the last seventeen years of his career at Princeton, where he was chairman of the department of theology.

DeHaan was a good student, retaining what he heard, and got his lessons in short order, according to Edward Tanis.

Summers during seminary days Dr. DeHaan pastored

small churches — in 1923 he had a charge north of Holland, and in 1924 he served in Lafayette, Ind. The first year he hammered hard at modernism, an issue of growing concern in the '20s, and the following summer he preached almost exclusively from the Heidelberg catechism.

When he graduated in the spring of 1925, his family proudly watched, including his mother and father,* who thanked God that they at last had a full-fledged pastor-son.

It was a devoted Reformed man — though with a Scofield Bible and a leaning toward premillennialism — who assumed the pastorate of the established, flourishing Calvary Reformed Church on Fulton Street in Grand Rapids.

Both his parents were justifiably proud of their son, for he quickly began to attract large audiences. He was a good preacher, too, sound in doctrine, and a man deeply concerned with bringing lost sheep into the fold. He had a booming voice, unaided by electronic equipment.

Among those God drew to himself through Martin's strong evangelistic preaching was Ada, his sister by adoption. She considered herself a Christian because she had learned the catechism and was a church member. But when she joined the crowds who flocked to Calvary Reformed Church to hear her brother, she became increasingly uneasy; it seemed that his eyes were on her, almost to the extent of searching out her soul. Yet in one visit he greeted her following a service, saying, "Why, Ada, I didn't know you were here."

At home on Sunday afternoons, she listened to Martin preach on the radio. The more she heard him, the more she doubted her salvation. He made it so clear that being a church member did not necessarily mean that an individual belonged to God's family. She vowed not to listen, but Sundays her hand fell on the radio dial, and on came the

*[Reitze himself had made a clear-cut profession of faith in 1921. The godly Johanna lived only a year after Martin became a minister, dying September 6, 1926, at the age of 60, a victim of diabetes. Reitze lived on to the age of 72, dying after a brief illness on November 8, 1931.]

71

deep, persuasive voice of her brother. Finally one Sunday afternoon in March, 1927, she said yes to Jesus Christ there beside her radio — she was depending wholly on Him for the eternal salvation of her spirit and not on works that she had done.

Maynard Vander Zaag was another convert during Calvary Reformed days. "Minnerd, if anything happens to you I'll figure it's my fault," Doc told his ex-driver one day, putting his arm around him. "I set you a pretty poor example."

Vander Zaag shook his head "no," though in reality he had looked up to the doctor in earlier days. Now he was seeing the new Doc in action.

Subsequently, in a service at Calvary Reformed, he placed his faith solely in the Saviour. "I was one of those stiff church people up to that point," he recalls. "Doc helped me see what Jesus Christ was all about."

Exciting things were happening in Grand Rapids, to be sure. On November 18, 1926, the DeHaans welcomed their fourth child and second son, Marvin. This was frosting on the cake of what was becoming a significant ministry.

In a marked manner the Spirit "turned on" Calvary Reformed Church under Martin DeHaan. Because of the increased attendance, a building program was launched. People came early to get seats. There were no gimmicks. The only extra attraction besides solid evangelistic preaching was a half-hour of congregational singing that warmed up early arrivals awaiting the regular service.

On Monday evenings, in addition to the midweek meeting, the aggressive pastor taught Bible classes — from 7 to 8 o'clock for teenagers, and 8 to 9 for adults. He took both groups deep into the Word of God, making once-dry portions come alive. Teens and adults alike looked upon him as the voice of authority, and youths loved him despite his strict ways.

Often on Friday evenings, during his Reformed pastorate, Dr. DeHaan himself attended a Bible class, termed the "largest weekday class in the world," at the Mel Trotter

Mission. Here he added to his knowledge of the Word as he heard Dr. Billy McCarrell, pastor of Cicero Bible Church near Chicago. Regularly some 2,000 people, including the mayor of Grand Rapids, filled the former theater building, with its three balconies, to hear the fundamental and hidden truths of the Bible expounded by the colorful, veteran teacher. DeHaan and McCarrell became warm friends through their common interest in the Bible.

As the voice and style of preaching of M. R. DeHaan became even better known in the Grand Rapids area, another service was added on Sunday evenings at Calvary Reformed — an after-service for those from other churches. "Informality and freedom prevailed, but without fanaticism and disorder. Many made decisions for Christ," Dirk De Pree recalls. "There was a deep moving of the Holy Spirit. This continued for several years. These were the days that the Doctor became a powerful preacher and teacher of the Word, and a widely known personality."

DeHaan moved about the platform freely, crashing his fist onto the pulpit frequently to punctuate a thought, his deep voice and exciting messages riveting listeners to their seats. He once became literally lost in communion with God during the "long prayer" just prior to the sermon. When he finished he opened his eyes and found himself looking at the organ pipes behind the pulpit, his back to the audience. "This was so embarrassing that from then on when I prayed I always held on to the pulpit," DeHaan said to a friend later on.

In his years at Calvary Reformed, he increasingly sought to explore the depths of the Word of God, not being content merely to preach what he had learned in seminary. The brilliant attorney-turned-pastor C. I. Scofield "tutored" him through his reference Bible.

During this period, Dr. DeHaan also feasted on the Bible teaching of such men as William L. Pettingill, H. A. Ironside, James M. Gray, and William R. Newell.

It was the late Dr. Pettingill, one of the editors of the Scofield Reference Bible, to whom Dr. DeHaan gave credit for straightening him out on the relationship of law and grace. Pettingill, preaching at the invitation of DeHaan, declared that salvation had nothing to do with observance of the law. The law, he said, speaks of condemnation and judgment but has nothing to do with changing the heart. It's the grace of God that gives life. Grace plus nothing equals salvation, the visiting preacher emphasized. Afterward, DeHaan, who had been reared on a strong dose of the Ten Commandments, approached him. "One of us is wrong, and if it's me I want to know it," he said. Pettingill shared with him the booklet *Rightly Dividing the Word of Truth*** by Scofield, and it was the beginning of what DeHaan deemed a clearer understanding of the doctrines of law and grace.

He stepped up his evangelistic appeal, and about the same time began to stir his people concerning the imminent return of Christ for His Church. "This same Jesus, who came 1900 years ago, may return at any moment," he declared. "His second coming is mentioned 240 times in the New Testament alone, more times by far than any other doctrine in the entire Bible. The exact day of this great event, however, has not been revealed."

Many listeners dared not leave the services before making sure of their relationship to God. Some wept and agonized before they had assurance that they were saved and would be among those caught up to be with the Lord.

They wanted to be with Christ, reigning, when He set up His millennial kingdom upon the earth, for Dr. DeHaan thundered that, according to the clear teachings of Scripture, the coming again of the Lord Jesus Christ would not be the end of the world. "The end of the *age* and the end of the *world* are two entirely different events, separated by a great period of time," he explained. "The end of the world will not occur until at least 1,000 years after the end of this

*Still in print, exactly as written, available through Zondervan.

present age. The end of the *age* will come when our Lord returns for His Church. After a brief period of tribulation, He will cleanse the earth and judge His enemies. Then, our Lord will set up His messianic, millennial kingdom upon the earth and the saints will reign with Him."

A number of Christians in western Michigan had already been introduced to this view, but to thousands of others, Dr. DeHaan preached of things to come that were excitingly new.

That this sensational brand of preaching should come from a Reformed man disturbed local leaders in the denomination. While here and there a few Reformed pastors, in the tradition of some of the Holland pioneers, held views similar to DeHaan's, they were quieter about it. Most Reformed men of the area differed sharply with DeHaan, the pretribulation premillennialist. Though they seldom preached on the doctrine, to them the millennium would not be a literal thousand-year reign of Christ on earth as DeHaan believed Revelation 20 states. Some Reformed men believed the millennium should be thought of as the present state of the righteous in Heaven; others interpreted it as being the peace enjoyed by Christians on earth; and, still others, that it represents the entire period from the cross, when Satan was defeated, until the return of Christ. Whatever their varying views on the millennium, the amillennialists held that the return of the Lord from Heaven would result in a general resurrection, judgment, then eternity. To DeHaan, all of this was a "cancerous curse" of Bible teaching growing out of "spiritualizing Scriptures."

However, DeHaan's views on another subject — infant baptism — brought the outspoken Calvary pastor to the point of an official Church spanking. It all began rather quietly behind the scenes as the pastor compared Reformed doctrine on baptism with other views, and with what he felt the Bible taught on the subject. Reformed or covenant theology, he observed, declares that in the Church age infant baptism replaces infant circumcision. Since, according to Reformed doctrine, the Church is the Israel of the New Testament, God's covenant community is expected faithfully to present their children for baptism so that they can be true children of the Abrahamic covenant (Genesis 12, 13, 15, and 17) and heirs of the promise of God's blessings.

DeHaan visited several of his Reformed colleagues to discuss the matter. "I can't find anything in the Bible that comes close to suggesting that I should baptize infants," he asserted. Some of the men indicated it was primarily a dedication, but DeHaan countered, "Then why use water?"

The matter became more serious when the Calvary pastor ignored the Reformed calendar and did not preach on infant baptism when the subject was scheduled to be discussed from the pulpit. Church officers mentioned the matter to him, but did not seem unduly alarmed; the calendar wasn't compulsory, though usually followed.

Then one day a couple asked Dr. DeHaan to baptize their baby. He frankly told them his views had changed, and that he could not in good conscience do so.

In later years he was to write what he in essence told the couple: "The Bible does not contain anything whatsoever concerning this subject. There is no record in the Bible where babies were ever baptized, much less sprinkled. . . . God promises in His Word that if we will 'train up a child in the way he should go, when he is old he will not depart from it' (Proverbs 22:6). We have a right to claim God's promises for our children, but they certainly are not saved because they are born of Christian parents, or because they have been sprinkled as babies, nor are they covenant children; but they must come to a personal knowledge and acceptance of the Lord Jesus Christ as their own personal Savior."

Commenting further on the matter, Dr. DeHaan declared: "I believe that all children who die before the age of accountability are saved, since they have never had the opportunity of rejecting the Gospel of the Lord Jesus Christ or the light that God has given to them. We believe that Jesus died on

76

the cross of Calvary for the sins of mankind, and today only one sin can condemn a man, and that is the sin of willfully rejecting the message which God gives to fallen man. I believe with all my heart that every baby that dies, whether before birth or after birth, before it reaches the age of accountability, goes to Heaven."

With the matter of infant baptism in the open, he met with his church consistory to explain his position. He explained that he had studied the subject at length, looking both into the Bible and into writings of many theologians, and praying much about the matter. He simply could not see that baptism of infants had taken the place of circumcision. He believed only in believer's baptism, speaking of one's personal relationship to Jesus Christ and symbolizing the believer's death and resurrection with Christ.

Though most of the Calvary consistory sided with Dr. DeHaan and his non-Reformed views on the matter, the announcement proved a bombshell, especially after the pastor shared his beliefs with the entire congregation on Sunday morning.

At this point, Martin DeHaan had gone too far, cried the Grand Rapids Classis of the Reformed Church in America. Frisians, from whom he had descended, are said to be *stiff koppen* (bullheaded), and he had a bad case of it, the Classis charged in so many words.

As the ecclesiastical wheels ground toward an official censure, the DeHaans sensed that their days indeed were numbered within the Reformed Church.

These were extremely dark days for M. R. DeHaan, but God had a bright future for him.

7

And the word of the Lord was published throughout all the region. *Acts 13:49*

A Thriving New Church

Although most members of the congregation had known that a break was coming, the official announcement was made on Sunday, March 3, 1929, at the morning service of Calvary Reformed Church. Parishioners filled the sanctuary early and sat through the early part of the service expectantly awaiting the pastor's comments on the brief announcement that appeared in the church bulletin. Seventeen members of the consistory had resigned, and their names were listed. A hush fell over the congregation as Dr. DeHaan began his announcements.

"You have read in the bulletin the notice concerning the resignation of 17 members of the consistory," he began in his full deep voice. "These men have not only resigned from Calvary Reformed Church but also from the Reformed Church in America. They have organized a new church which will be known as the Calvary Undenominational Church. These men comprise the new board. They have called me to be pastor of the new church and I have accepted. Beginning Wednesday evening of this coming week we will hold our first service in the building formerly occupied by the Orpheum Theatre on lower Monroe Avenue."

A 20-inch account the next day in the *Grand Rapids Press* spelled out details of this newest development in the dramatic ever-changing story of the outspoken pastor and his 17 consistorymen. Asked by the *Press* writer if he considered that the step removed him and his consistory from the jurisdiction of the Reformed Church, he answered, "Absolutely." When the reporter suggested that the position of the Classis might be contrary to his, DeHaan asserted, "The consistory and I are out of the Reformed denomination."

As the case of the Reformed Church in America vs. M. R. DeHaan came to a conclusion, and as DeHaan began his ministry as pastor of Calvary Undenominational Church, he spoke with love toward those with whom he so sharply differed. "I love them and know them to be sincere and honest. I still love the Reformed Church. I shall continue to love her. I shall pray for her that God may bless her. I cannot agree in all things with the brethren, but even after I am out I shall stand ready to aid and assist in any way I can in the spiritual welfare of the organization. I have no personal grievance against any individual. I believe they are wrong but will love them as brethren. . . ."

The first midweek meeting of Calvary Undenominational Church on March 6 attracted representatives and entire family groups that had pulled out, all but filling the auditorium of the Orpheum Theater building. Such enthusiasm was to continue, due largely to the powerful preaching and teaching of M. R. DeHaan.

This first service is graphically described by Grand Rapids

upholstery dealer Lewis Steenwyk, then 21 and present with his father and mother:

"Dr. DeHaan preached on what will take place on the earth after the rapture of the church. And, of course, he had people thumbing through their Bibles, looking up this reference, then that reference. My dad sat there and looked them up, and held the Bible right under my nose so I could read them too. Though I'm not emotionally inclined, I was really shook up. I had a struggle within. I knew what a lost sinner I was, and I was just simply miserable.

"When the invitation was given I said to myself, 'If these other people want to make fools of themselves and raise their hands and go forward in a meeting, let them do it. I'm not going to make a fool of myself.' So I sat there. During the course of the invitation it seemed to me as if someone up in the balcony above us reached down and lifted my hand, against my stubborn will. When Dr. DeHaan saw it, he said, 'God bless you, young man.' Just that quickly the tension was gone and there was peace. I went forward.

"After the service Dr. DeHaan opened the Bible with me and read Romans 10:9 and 10 — 'If thou shalt confess with thy mouth the Lord Jesus, and shalt believe in thine heart that God hath raised Him from the dead, thou shalt be saved. For with the heart man believeth unto righteousness; and with the mouth confession is made unto salvation.' Surely I believed that and that was it. So I owe Dr. DeHaan a great debt of gratitude for leading me to the Lord Jesus Christ."

Lewis Steenwyk recalls many memorable details of the first years of Calvary Undenominational Church:

— "We transferred the radio facilities from the Reformed Church to the theater and continued on the air. The six-and-three-quarters-hour broadcasts on radio every Sunday had a tremendous listening audience. Between the Mel Trotter Mission (with its teaching on the second coming of Christ) and Calvary Undenominational (with the speakers* that Dr. DeHaan brought there and his messages on the pre-millennial return of the Lord), we had a revival here in Grand Rapids. Tremendous! We didn't call it that; we didn't know what a revival was — the word was new to many of us. But the church was packed Sunday morning and night. People were being saved all over. Street meetings were being held. Our young people's group thought nothing of having 150-200 out on Monday night for a Bible class with Dr. DeHaan as teacher. The main youth activities centered around the Monday Bible Class, a street meeting on Tuesday evenings in the Negro section of the city, prayer meeting on Wednesday, and a Saturday night street meeting. Many of the young people are today full-time ministers for the Lord.

— "Our Sunday evening services at Calvary Church began at 6:45 o'clock with a song service, and we did not have much special music. Dr. DeHaan kept it down to a minimum. He was a long-winded preacher, and many times would still be going at 9:15. When he gave the salvation invitation, it was not at all unusual to see people come down the aisles and go to the prayer rooms, where personal workers counseled with them.

— "Dr. DeHaan's success and his power as a preacher was that he accepted the Word of God as verbally inspired. He did not believe in spiritualizing the Scriptures. He believed in taking the Bible literally.

—"A verse that was strong with Dr. DeHaan was 2 Timothy 2:15 — he believed in 'rightly dividing the word of truth,' as the verse says. I can remember him saying many times that there are three classes of people — Jew, Gentile, and the Church of God. When unbelieving Jews become believers, they become members of the Church, Dr. DeHaan

*Among them: Dr. Arno C. Gaebelein, Dr. William L. Pettingill, Dr. Donald Grey Barnhouse, Dr. Albert Hughes, Dr. L. Sale-Harrison, Dr. Norman B. Harrison, Dr. Louis Talbot and Dr. William McCarrell.

82

pointed out. When unbelieving Gentiles become believers they too become members of the Church. So there are three groups. Dr. DeHaan urged us to read the Bible and consider to whom the Holy Spirit is speaking. Unbelieving Gentiles in the Old Testament? Unbelieving Jews? Or is it written to the Church, the body of believers? If you follow that line, that method of interpretation, Dr. DeHaan pointed out, you'll not be calling the Church *Israel*.

— "He didn't believe in accepting the blessings of Israel and forgetting the curses, as he had learned in the Reformed Church. They believe the Church is spiritual Israel. Well, Dr. DeHaan used to say if we are under the Abrahamic covenant, as they believe, then we had better start over to Palestine and get our share of the Promised Land, as God promised Abraham that to his seed He would give all this land 'from the river of Egypt unto the great river Euphrates for an everlasting possession.'"

Calvary Undenominational met in the old Orpheum Theater building until the summer of 1929, then moved to the St. Cecilia building, pending the completion of a new building. On January 26, 1930, the congregation of some 700 members moved to new quarters at Michigan Street and College Avenue, N. E., an impressive rambling structure, boasting a new auditorium and a renovated former elementary school.

Calvary Church stepped up its program, attracting greater crowds than ever. The auditorium seated around 2000, and often chairs were brought in to accommodate others.

Dr. DeHaan recognized the radio ministry as probably the greatest outstanding domestic missionary work of his church. "This work is definitely blessed in a peculiar way by God for the conversion of sinners, the edification of saints, and the comfort of the shut-ins," stated the church dedication booklet. "Our radio ministry brings to an unseen audience four services each Lord's Day. At 10 o'clock in the morning we broadcast our regular Sunday morning worship. At 2 in the afternoon we present the radio request program.

83

At 6:45 in the evening, our regular evening evangelistic service, and at 10 at night, a good-night hour of fellowship and heart-to-heart talk."

Dr. DeHaan "gave the Word like medicine," as some termed it, recalling his years as a practicing physician. Zealously, he sometimes, to the embarrassment of some, and to the amusement of others, pounded the pulpit vigorously, in his enthusiasm throwing a leg over it Billy Sunday-style.

In making his sermons relevant to the times, Dr. DeHaan borrowed ideas from editorial columns of newspapers. The *Grand Rapids Herald* posed the question, "What is wrong with our educational system?" and the Calvary pastor fired back from the pulpit with the sure remedy. "It ignores the missing link. The editor says, 'Somewhere in our educational system is a weak link.' Ah, no, not a weak one, but a missing one! No system, economic, political, or educational, can prosper that ignores the sovereignty of God's will and the existence of One who will judge all things by His Son, Jesus Christ."

In his message De Haan took sharp issue with Leslie A. Butler, superintendent of the Grand Rapids public schools, who had declared that "as education increases, crime decreases." Butler quoted statistics showing that 90 per cent of the inmates of a Michigan prison never received an education above the sixth grade. "Such jumping at conclusions," said DeHaan, "alarms us, especially when it comes from an educator like Mr. Butler. There is no foundation for the statement that 'as education increases, crime decreases.' The reverse is true. During the past 15 years, education has gone ahead by leaps and bounds, and crime has kept up a commensurate pace. . . . Education has done nothing to retard the unwavering increase of wickedness in the human heart. . . . We attack man in the wrong place; the trouble is with the heart and not the head.

"There was a time not so many years ago when, in the school system of this land, God was recognized and the Bible was revered and taught. They were days of God's blessing on this fair land. But gradually the devil plied his trade until God has been thrust out of the schools and the Bible either banished or put alongside of any other secular book for the study of literature or history. . . . Putting the Bible back in school is the cure for educational problems!"

The hand of God obviously was on M. R. DeHaan. Like Peter of old, he preached with great power and people were "pricked in their hearts." But he was just as interested in talking to one or two persons as to a crowd. He had time for people. He enjoyed visiting with Maynard Vander Zaag, his ex-driver, and liked to roughhouse as in days gone by. "I kind of like you, Minnerd," he would say, putting his arm around him and rubbing his hand in Maynard's face. Then a wrestling match began on the living room floor, much to the distress of Mrs. Vander Zaag.

When Dr. DeHaan learned that a son had been born to the Vander Zaags, he visited the home and remarked, "He's certainly a fine boy. Let's give him back to the Lord." And he proceeded to pray a dedicatory prayer right there. The Vander Zaags today firmly believe that God answered that prayer, for their son Bob gave himself to the Lord's service and now pastors a church in California.

At weddings Dr. DeHaan exhorted couples at length on the need for making Christ the center of their homes and teaching their children to follow in the ways of God. "He exhorted us at our wedding," remembers Lewis Steenwyk, "and, as I recall it, he laid special emphasis on going to the Lord with our problems."

In the late '30s Calvary members whispered of problems within the church. Trouble broke openly as Dr. DeHaan returned one day in May, 1938, from a week's meetings in another city and discovered that three men on the board, who also comprised the music committee, had fired Floyd D. Leary, who had been director of music and young people's work. Irked, DeHaan in clear, well-chosen terms tongue-lashed the offending board members. On Sunday,

May 15, he called a special congregational meeting for the following Tuesday. At the session he exhorted the membership to give Leary a vote of confidence, which they did, and Leary, who had offered to resign, agreed to continue serving.

Still infuriated with his board, Dr. DeHaan asked the congregation to declare the recent election of deacons and elders void. The majority responded by voting in favor of the request, and furthermore gave the pastor authority to appoint a committee to replace the board until the next annual meeting in March, 1939.

As an upshot of the matter, six men, five of them ex-members, took legal action, obtaining an injunction on Dr. DeHaan and the committee of five he had appointed to conduct church business. It was served on Friday, May 20.

The following Sunday, May 22, Dr. DeHaan resigned. On Monday, Dr. DeHaan was quoted by the *Herald* as resigning for two reasons: "health and conscience. I have conscientious scruples about going to law about a church matter, and because of these scruples and the condition of my health I have resigned. I have no plans at present, except to regain my health if possible."

Indeed, Dr. DeHaan had been ill for much of the spring, being absent from the pulpit for all but two of 16 Sundays. His son Richard, then 15, years later in a series of radio messages on "Men Sent From God," recalled the trying days:

"I do rejoice in recounting those happy seasons of revival blessing [at Calvary Undenominational Church]; however, there are some things I wish I could forget: events which have made an indelible mark and impression upon my life and which loom up before me today as a terrible nightmare. Oh, that I could erase them from my mind forever. For while the work of a pastor can be most satisfying and rewarding, it also involves extremely difficult, trying, discouraging, and disappointing experiences. The misunderstandings, the false accusations, and the opposition, especially from those within the church, can sap the energy, break the spirit, and frustrate the efforts of even the most dedicated servant.

"Even now, I can visualize my dad slumped down in a chair sobbing out his heart to God. I can still feel the quickening of my own pulse as time after time he found it necessary to excuse himself from the evening meals due to nervous exhaustion. How his countenance changed during those days of adversity and difficulty. He began to stoop under the heavy load until almost broken in spirit, and physically exhausted, his weary heart rebelled. Arriving home from school one day, I saw him lying on the davenport, his face contorted, spelling out the severe pain in his chest, brought on by the tension, the extreme burdens and pressures of a conscientious ministry."

From his sickbed Dr. DeHaan, writing for the April 10, 1938, church bulletin, blamed his illness on "multitudinous cares and responsibilities of the work of the church, spiritual, financial, missionary, radio and local." He urged the congregation to pray for him and be faithful "in regard to these matters. These are stressing days," he continued. "A great recession is on. But to God's people a recession is a challenge — not a signal to lie down."

The heart seizure in the spring of 1938 was Dr. DeHaan's second. He had suffered his first, a mild attack, in 1936.

Now, following his bombshell of May 22, 1938, he was a depressed, sick man — a pastor without a job. (Some years later, a Calvary Church committee sought to bring about a peaceful settlement of the matter. This resulted in renewed fellowship, and Dr. DeHaan subsequently preached from the Calvary pulpit in a guest role.)

Paul and Barnabas had clashed and separated over John Mark in the matter of his joining their missionary team; Dr. DeHaan had clashed with brethren over a member of his staff and "departed asunder one from the other." Paul chose Silas, and Barnabas selected Mark, and the Holy Spirit used both teams; likewise, God chose to continue blessing Calvary

Church, and He had a great worldwide ministry ahead for
M. R. DeHaan.

8

Behold, I have set before thee an open door, and no man can shut it; for thou hast a little strength, and hast kept my word, and hast not denied my name. *Revelation 3:8*

A 50-Watt Beginning

A short while after he left the pulpit of Calvary Undenominational Church, Dr. DeHaan met for lunch in Detroit with his friend Dr. Billy McCarrell, the Illinois pastor whose Bible classes DeHaan had attended in Grand Rapids. "I really got a good sock on the schnozzle," he told McCarrell. The physician-pastor recounted the events leading to his resignation.

McCarrell, in Detroit to teach a Bible class, leaned forward and looked DeHaan squarely in the eye. "Doctor, God has given you a great gift in Bible teaching. Perhaps He is opening the door to a new type of ministry for you."

Even while struggling to regain his health in 1938, DeHaan

had been faithfully teaching several weekday Bible classes, sometimes showing up to teach when the average man might have stayed home in bed. On Monday nights he conducted a class in Flint, Mich.; Tuesday nights, Buffalo, N.Y.; Thursday nights, Grand Rapids; Friday nights, Detroit; and Saturday nights, East Detroit. His popularity was widespread. Thousands tuned in to hear him on the now extinct Michigan Radio Network. He taught with authority, making the way of salvation through God's grace plain, and exciting spiritual pulses with lessons on prophecy. He was a teacher who knew the hidden mysteries of the Bible. As a result, it was common to find more than 1,000 persons at many of the weekday sessions.

Little did Billy McCarrell know how much of a prophet he was the day he suggested that perhaps God had a Bible-teaching ministry for M. R. DeHaan. And certainly DeHaan had no inkling that the Sunday morning he broadcast live for the first time on radio station WEXL, a 50-watt outlet in Royal Oak, a Detroit suburb, it marked the beginning of a lifetime Bible-teaching ministry that would reach around the world. The program was called The Detroit Bible Class.

The format of the half-hour broadcast was simple. Elmer and Maynard Oppenhuizen, whom Dr. DeHaan imported from Grand Rapids, opened and closed the broadcast singing "Tell Me The Story of Jesus." Later, in 1939, Doctor decided that a trio would add to the program, and he asked Henry Bosch, a baritone who was on radio himself in Grand Rapids, to join the Oppenhuizen brothers. Occasionally Dr. DeHaan, with informality characteristic of those early broadcasts would join the trio and make it a quartet by adding his raspy bass.

In the early years there was no rehearsal in the studio. A Salvation Army Band played a concert immediately preceding the DeHaan broadcast, and as the station announcer made the station break, the bandsmen raced out of the studio and the DeHaan team hurried in, all within the space of a minute. Mrs. Elmer Oppenhuizen would hardly be seated at the organ when the red light came on signaling the trio to begin singing.

Often several members of the DeHaan family accompanied the Doctor to the station. Richard, who years later was to succeed his father on the broadcast, has hazy recollections of the early days. He was 15 when the program began and recalls that the entire family was thrilled at the response and the way the program grew in its outreach.

One staff member recalls Richard and Marv, then mischievous boys, leaning from a window in the CKLW* studios high above the Detroit River, trying to spit on objects below and sailing paper airplanes.

But even these two livewire PKs were ultimately to have a part in the growing outreach of the radio ministry.

Fully convinced by 1941 that God had indeed called him to a career in gospel broadcasting, DeHaan set up headquarters in Grand Rapids. At this point he changed the name from Detroit Bible Class to Radio Bible Class, the new name being more fitting because of a wider outreach.

When DeHaan began to organize in Grand Rapids, he hired a fledgling secretary, Leona Hertel, daughter of a close friend of Priscilla's. She held the Doctor in awe, having since the age of 12 attended Bible classes he taught. One day she pumped up courage to ask for the day off to compete in a swimming meet. He smiled and nodded. "OK, just so you win!" She did. And for the rest of his life, during the next 24 years, she was to continue obeying his commands.

Meantime, the two boys Richard and Marvin, were pitching in more and more as the work increased, running the press in the basement, doing janitor work, licking stamps. Priscilla DeHaan also helped in the office. "I remember very well the day we had $85.00 in the bank to pay bills. It was a big day," she recalls.

It was with great enthusiasm that Dr. DeHaan picked up the mail when he was home. Oldtime employees remember his delight in doing so, whistling, joking, talking, and

*50,000-watt outlet (Windsor/Detroit), from which the program later originated.

thanking God for sending in the means to continue broadcasting. This evidence that God's hand was on him in the radio ministry not only strengthened his faith but it proved good therapy for his body as his health steadily improved, enabling him to work long hours and fill an increasing number of preaching and teaching engagements.

Both boys, blessed with deep voices like their father's, got their chances to help with the broadcast itself. When Richard was about 18 he did the opening announcement, offered the sermon booklet, and closed the program. Marv announced for the first time when he was 15, subbing for the absent Rich, and continued to do so when he was needed, until he became too involved with medical school.

From the beginning on 50-watt WEXL, DeHaan published sermon booklets, including in them the radio messages. Later, in 1956 the monthly *Our Daily Bread* devotional booklet was added, with Dr. DeHaan and Henry Bosch as coeditors.

Naturally, the printing of the sermon booklets and, later, the devotional guides, plus radio time, needed regular and heavy support. DeHaan, full of both faith and conservative good sense, often said, "If the Lord wants us to go ahead, He'll supply the money. If He doesn't send it in, that'll be our signal to quit broadcasting."

If a new staff member suggested that gimmicks be employed to step up contributions, DeHaan squelched him immediately. "We'll never use come-ons like sand from Palestine or rain water that fell into the Jordan," the Doctor said more than once.

Instead, he depended on God to "incline the hearts of Thy people to send the money."

Dr. DeHaan considered his class members the finest people in the world. And he sensed their prayers as he ministered. He often spoke in these terms:

"We thank God for the thousands of you dear saints of God who intercede for us in our work of broadcasting the Gospel. Praying is, after all, the greatest thing you can do for us. I am convinced that if it were not for you, the unseen host of unnoticed pray-ers, the devil would have had the program of the Radio Bible Class off the air long ago."

Dr. DeHaan himself prayed fervently for the ministry God had given him. Then, both figuratively and sometimes literally, he rolled up his sleeves and expounded the Word till perspiration poured from his body.

To Dr. DeHaan, there was nothing more thrilling than to lean forward before a microphone and expound the wonders of the Bible. Whether taping a message or teaching on a live broadcast, he taught almost as if he could see his vast audience, occasionally interjecting such a comment as, "I'll repeat that Bible reference — I think someone missed it." He thought of his listeners as taking notes and thumbing through their Bibles with him as he taught.

While there were some who could not take his gravel voice, true DeHaan fans considered it an asset. There was a certain mellowness despite the raspiness, but above all he spoke with conviction and with the authority of one who had just come from a private audience with God.

"The Lord used that voice with its distinctive quality," says Richard, "to be sort of a trademark. When folk once heard it, there was no mistaking it when they ran across it again on the dial. After a few words, there was no doubt: 'That's the man.' The Lord used his voice. In fact, some have written since his home-going that they miss the 'sweetest voice in radio!'"

"At one time, the Doctor had a voice somewhat like Richard's — deep and mellow and mild," recalls Mrs. DeHaan. "In the early days of his evangelistic fervor he preached in tent meetings and at other gatherings without the aid of public-address systems, and it was very hard on his voice."

Marvin DeHaan, speaking as a physician, speculates that in those early days the voice developed its gruff qualities from chronic laryngitis. The vocal cords, he believes, became inflamed and the constant irritation caused the cords to thicken.

"It never really bothered him particularly," recalls Marvin, thinking back to the beginning years of the Radio Bible Class. "He would complain when he would lose his voice or it would be very poor. He used to gargle a lot. Hot salt water. And I mean hot — he never did anything halfway. Whatever you do, do it right, was his philosophy."

In the summer of 1946 when Dr. DeHaan was doing a live radio program, sudden pain struck him in the chest and arms. His voice faltered, but few listeners noticed. With beads of perspiration on his forehead and his face gripped in pain, he finished the broadcast. Staff workers rushed to him and a doctor was called. M. R. DeHaan had suffered a severe heart attack. For months to come, his personality would be missing from the airwaves.

Teaching the Bible class

9

Go ye into all the world, and preach the gospel
to every creature. *Mark 16:15*

A Worldwide Ministry

When Dr. DeHaan had his heart attack in 1946 and was
out of action for several months, there was one bright side
to the matter: his broadcast would continue uninterrupted,
for he had a capable substitute in the person and voice of
his tall, manly son, Richard.

Feeling God's call to become a minister, Richard had entered Northern Baptist Seminary, Chicago, in 1944 after
attending Calvin College and doing further work at Wheaton
College. His father's heart attack occurred during the summer months, so Richard stepped in immediately, and did not
return to seminary until a year later. Previously he had been

attending classes four days a week in Chicago, then working with his father on Saturdays, Sundays, and Mondays.

It had been an open secret that Dr. DeHaan had been grooming Richard for the day when he would fill in as teacher, with the plan of his someday taking over the broadcast.

Thus, as in 1946 Richard stepped in for his ailing father, the elder DeHaan was thankful to God for his willing substitute. Richard filled in until the Doctor was strong enough to again take his place at the microphone. Old-timers have never forgotten the first broadcast made after his heart attack. Speaking from his bed at home, with an emotion-filled and trembling voice, he thanked his audience for their prayers, and for the way they had stood by the work during his recovery.

The Radio Bible Class radio program has always been the backbone of the DeHaan ministry. And it was here that M. R. was in his element, whether broadcasting or speaking with conviction to make a point to an associate regarding the wisdom of adding certain stations or dropping other outlets. He periodically spent hours reviewing the radio log, culling out the undesirable stations, and seeking better time spots. He believed in spending Radio Bible Class dollars as wisely as possible, reaching the most people at the least expense.

And, as DeHaan and his staff prayed, God opened doors. In time, the Radio Bible Class with the voice of M. R. De Haan was reaching millions through hundreds of strategically located stations across the U.S., Canada, and in many foreign lands.

From the station manager's viewpoint, Radio Bible Class has a good format. It's not "hillbilly," as men in the trade classify some religious broadcasts. It has class.

Because of M. R. DeHaan's successful formula, other broadcasters journeyed to Grand Rapids to learn from him. They recognized him not only as an able Bible teacher but as an astute businessman. "How do you handle your mail so efficiently? How do you carry on a printing operation and send out so much literature with so few people?" These were among the questions.

The answers were there as they talked with M. R. DeHaan, and as he showed them the Radio Bible Class operation. They saw that, in his wisdom, Dr. DeHaan had surrounded himself with capable people. Visitors chatting with veteran employees such as Henry Bosch would have heard: "Dr. DeHaan hires consecrated people and has kept a good spirit going. He has always said, 'Remember, this is not primarily a business; this is a ministry! We must be businesslike, to be sure, but it's first of all a ministry.' He has taught us to do things 'as unto the Lord.'"

Though the gruff exterior of the founder of RBC frightened his secretary when she began working for him in the early years, and afterward sent shivers down other spines, employees who overlooked his severity found his door and heart wide open to them. These were his children, and he played his role as father in excellent fashion.

One girl, a part-time worker, came to him to seek counsel regarding her career. Should she continue with school or go to work immediately in the Lord's service? He strongly advised her to prepare herself and not follow her emotions.

He enjoyed giving certain employees nicknames. For some reason he called a girl named Margaret by the name Sarah, pleasing her no end. He shared bits of humor with the staff as he walked about the plant, his hands in his back pockets. He enjoyed theological discussions with the men at coffee break, sometimes giving a ten-minute Bible message while drinking extra strong coffee so hot that the fellows "thought steam would come out his ears," as one man put it.

Whenever the Doctor was in town, he met with the office staff for their regular morning chapel services. Often he shared messages planned for radio. He periodically reminded employees that they were rendering a service to the Lord, that they were in a real sense, missionaries. "When you think of missions, think of the Radio Bible Class," he urged.

In serious discussions with executives, DeHaan exhibited his strong convictions. If he believed something, he came to the point. Tact was not his strongest virtue. In earlier years, especially, he might crash his fist into his hand, or onto a desk, to punctuate his remarks. There were times when he was more like Simon than Peter. "I don't care! I want it done this way," he'd storm. (One close associate says in later years he largely got over this. When it did happen, "It would be only a little while and Doc would come out and say, 'I'm sorry; I don't know why I did that. I shouldn't have told you in that way. I should have been more kind.' He had a heart as big as a mountain," says the associate.)

An important milestone in the ministry of Radio Bible Class was passed in early 1958 when the Doctor dedicated to the Lord's service a new efficiently designed building. Conditions in an old windowless ex-theater building had become hopelessly overcrowded, forcing the conservative Doctor to build. For the first time both he and Richard had separate offices they could call their own.

The move failed to change DeHaan. He would walk about the sparkling, cheerful working area and say to an associate, "This thing is scaring me more than ever. I never envisioned this. I don't know why God ever picked me."

But God had a reason. In M. R. DeHaan He had a vessel He could use and get results.

Every mail brought evidence to Dr. DeHaan that his vigorous teaching was making an impact around the world. Besides the letters of thanks, there were the letters of no thanks. Even the latter ones, often filled with hate and scorn, brought a certain satisfaction to him. They usually amused him and gave him assurance that he was among the blessed of Luke 6:22, hated and reproached for the Lord's sake.

"You know, when you throw a stone at a pack of dogs,

the one that howls the loudest is the one that got hit," he philosophized. "I always feel that when they are howling I must have done something worthwhile. I must have hit them with the truth. When I preach I like to see people really become concerned, repent, and get saved. However, when I see some getting angry, I realize that this is also bound to happen. It's the opposite side of the two-edged sword of the Word."

When, in Dr. DeHaan's opinion, writers were really serious in their inquiries, he replied, usually within 24 hours. But when letters contained clever catch questions and traps he utterly ignored them. "There are so many people from whom we never hear a word unless they have a gripe or an argument, or something to criticize," he once said. "For these we keep a special file which we call the 'round file.' How I thank God for wastebaskets. What a labor-saving device they have proven to be. There are so many important things for the Christian to do that he cannot afford to waste time in unprofitable activities, arguments, debates, and discussions."

In replying to theological questions in the early years of Radio Bible Class, Dr. DeHaan believed he could answer any question that was asked him about the Bible. In later years this attitude changed. "I must admit that my ignorance of the Bible is most appalling," he wrote. "Over and over and over again I must tell people, 'My honest answer is: I don't know!' Sometimes I say, 'The best I can do is refer you to Deuteronomy 29:29' " [" . . . secret things belong unto the Lord our God. . . ."]

Though he had his opportunities, M. R. DeHaan never accepted any honorary degrees, preferring to let well enough alone and keep only the M.D. after his name. He kept up on medical advances to some degree through discussions with his physician son, Marvin, and by reading medical literature that continued coming to him. He offered certain medical advice in some of his writings and occasionally in messages, and thus in a loose sense he was still a practicing physician.

In his book, *Broken Things,* he wrote sagaciously concerning the relationship of physical disease to mental and spiritual health. He occasionally gave bits of medical advice in his *Our Daily Bread* writings. For example, lambasting "home remedies, worthless nostrums, cure-alls, diets, vitamins, minerals, salves, greases, and vibrators," making "the average medicine cabinet look like a miniature drugstore," he asserted: "Throw away 95% of those pills and gadgets . . . eat normal, balanced diets, quit worrying about . . . health, go to bed on time, and be more concerned with . . . spiritual health than the physical . . . [and] live longer and happier!"

At the office, Dr. DeHaan occasionally looked at sore throats, rashes, and the like. Once when Asian flu threatened Grand Rapids, he came to the office with his medical kit and gave all RBC employees a vaccine, resulting in only a minimum of absenteeism because of the disease.

Occasionally, when the call came, "Is there a doctor in the house?" DeHaan, the preacher-teacher, hurried to meet the emergency. While participating in an all-day church conference, he was interrupted in the midst of a sermon. "Quick! Come downstairs. A woman is dying!" Excusing himself, he left the pulpit and went to aid the victim. She had been helping prepare a meal and had sampled a piece of chicken, which became lodged in her throat. The woman was on her back and unconscious when Doctor arrived.

"I remembered what they had told me in medical school — in an emergency use emergency measures," DeHaan told an associate later. "So, because I had no instruments or anything, I put my fingers down her throat, tearing the tissue some because my fingers were too short for the job. I grabbed the piece of meat, then gave her resuscitation, and brought her back. She had an awfully sore throat because of it, but it saved her life."

Though DeHaan relished his sometime role of practicing physician, he often averred that he was not sorry he had left his medical career to preach the Gospel. Without doubt instances of his being God's obstetrician in thousands of spiritual births brought him greater joy than delivering babies as a country doctor.

There was the man who heard Dr. DeHaan one Sunday and later wrote, "Your message did something nothing else has ever done. I was drinking wine and beer in my room, and I heard that song, 'Do You Know Jesus?' and a memory came to me about Grand Rapids where I was born. I am a retired switchman. When I heard you I said, 'Well, here goes the works.' I knelt beside my bed and asked God to take me. I got up, got my wine and beer, and poured it down the drain. I ate my breakfast and prayed again. Doctor, pray for me. Please send me some books to help me live for God."

A Roman Catholic who had incurred the wrath of her church for marrying a divorced Protestant wrote Dr. DeHaan to tell him that his book *Revelation* had been instrumental in a great change in their spiritual lives. His pastor gave her husband the book, and he was restored to fellowship with the Lord through it, and she had committed her life to Christ. "We want to live for the Lord and hear all we can about His Word," she continued. "Thank you for the help your broadcasts and booklets have been to us."

Dr. Donald Johns, a Grand Rapids pediatrician, once gladdened the heart of Dr. DeHaan with the story related to him by a young father who, with his wife, had brought their baby in to him for treatment. Having discovered some Radio Bible Class booklets in the waiting room, the father said, "You know, Dr. DeHaan's ministry has had a real effect upon our home. When I was a child my parents came home one Sunday evening from a party, quarreling and arguing, and everything was going wrong. They turned on the radio and Dr. DeHaan was bringing a message. As they listened they realized that this was meant for them, and at the close of the program when Dr. DeHaan urged them to settle the question of their salvation *now*, they both got on their knees in the living room before the davenport, and accepted Christ as their own personal Savior. Their lives were changed, and our home was changed. Later on, my parents led me to the Lord, and I knelt in that same living room, before that same davenport, and asked the Lord to come into my heart and life."

On a visit to Tokyo, Dr. Johns met another man whose life is different today because of the ministry of M. R. DeHaan. The pediatrician sent this report to DeHaan: "Last night at the crusade meeting a Japanese pastor heard me introduced as being a doctor from Michigan, and very excitedly he sputtered out, 'I was saved through Dr. DeHaan's ministry. He baptized me in Washington.' Through your ministry he found Jesus Christ and now pastors a fundamental, evangelistic church here in Tokyo." He was referring to the Rev. Yutaka Akichika, who met Christ under Dr. DeHaan's ministry in 1939. Akichika's wife was converted through a Radio Bible Class broadcast some time later.

Commenting on the Japanese couple, Dr. DeHaan once wrote that there was no greater thrill to him than to see "his children" still walking in the truth years afterward. "There was a time early in my ministry that I often said, 'The greatest joy of a Christian is to lead a soul to Christ.' As the years passed, I changed my mind. . . . So many, over whom we rejoiced when they made their professions, soon fell by the wayside, and our joy came to ultimate grief and sorrow. But to come back to a place years afterward and find 'converts' growing in grace, walking in the truth — this is the greatest joy. And this is also Scriptural, for John says his greatest joy was "to hear that my children walk in truth."

"As I travel about the country my greatest joy is to meet, everywhere I go, folks who testify that ten, twenty, or thirty years ago they found Christ under my preaching," the Doctor declared in an issue of the Radio Bible Class *Newsletter* to members. "What a joy to receive letters in the mail constantly, telling us how years ago they were saved listening to the radio. A missionary writes from the field: 'I am here because of a sermon I heard you preach fourteen years ago, which resulted in the surrender of my life to Jesus.' A pastor in Washington, while introducing me at a CBMC banquet, told how, sitting at his radio sixteen years earlier he had been saved and dedicated his life to the ministry."

A classic example of a convert continuing to walk in truth concerns a Jewish woman who wrote that "God was good enough to open my eyes and ears to the marvelous fact that the Messiah did come to earth, and died on the cross for me." She wrote that a Christian friend mailed her "a pamphlet by Dr. DeHaan and informed me that her church was praying for Jews. I was astonished, for I didn't know anyone needed to pray for us," she continued. "Then I read the booklet and thought, *This isn't in my Bible.* I looked up the references and, sure enough, it was there. I started reading out of curiosity, and the more I read, the more God revealed His message to me. Every doubt and question was answered like magic. This all began ten months ago. Now my whole family has come to know Jesus. We have a Bible class in our home, and many of my bewildered Jewish friends are joining us. I listen to your broadcast on Sunday morning and receive a special blessing each time."

One of the most unusual cases on record at Radio Bible Class involves Robert Davis, an inmate at a penitentiary in Pennsylvania. In 1957 he wrote that "by chance" he had heard Dr. DeHaan on the radio and had read some of his messages. Facing the electric chair for murder, he wanted to be sure he knew the true meaning of salvation.

A letter and literature went out immediately. Then, in God's providence, the Rev. Henry Broersma, a visitation minister from Calvary Undenominational Church, Grand Rapids, dropped into the Radio Bible Class office and heard about the prisoner. "Wouldn't it be worth a trip to talk to him?" This triggered a series of circumstances that took him to the penitentiary, where he talked to the Death Row inmate shackled to two guards. Robert Davis indicated a trust in Jesus Christ during the counseling session. Later, he was granted a new trial and his death sentence was commuted to life in prison. But as he awaited trial he witnessed to other men and at least six more declared their trust in Christ and began studying God's Word.

A sequel to the conversion of Davis came when Broersma called again at the penitentiary and asked for Davis by his number. Presently, a guard brought a prisoner to him and said, "Here's your man." But it was not Robert Davis; it was a "wrong number." His name was Cleveland Thompson, he told the Christian worker. A conversation followed, and Thompson, the "wrong number," committed himself to Christ. Nine weeks later he walked to the electric chair, and within moments went into eternity, "absent from the body, present with the Lord."

Henry Broersma helped in another unusual case involving a young man serving time in a Michigan prison for negligent homicide. The mother of the victim wrote to the Radio Bible Class in early 1958 and asked that the staff pray with her for the prisoner's salvation. Gospel literature was sent and workers prayed. Later, the mother wrote, in part:

"On the evening of February 13 Rev. Broersma called to me the wonderful news — it had been his privilege that afternoon to lead the boy to the Lord. . . . What seems at the time like utter heartbreak to us is meant for our good, and is just part of something wonderful beyond compare that we'll understand fully in God's time.

". . . We had a letter from him this week. What a change it was from all previous letters! There was calm and peace and certainty and belief in Jesus Christ registered in this one. The others had always been more or less erratic, doubtful, somewhat fearful and confused, but not this last one! On two occasions he mentioned your booklets and expressed eagerness and pleasure in reading them. . . ."

One rewarding aspect of Doctor's ministry resulted from the fact that among listeners were many men of the clergy, preachers with small congregations on to evangelists with wide influence.

A well-known evangelist once said, "I have listened to him almost every Sunday for many years. A great deal of my Bible knowledge came from his teaching."

A Catholic priest once wrote that "for the past year or two I have been listening to you on the radio on Sunday mornings as I return from a sanatorium where I offer holy mass . . . and I think you are doing a great deal of good . . . and speak the truth without any human respect."

While people deeply affected by the Radio Bible Class ministry are vast in number and are found around the world, M. R. DeHaan never kept a record of results. "God keeps the records," he often said. But knowledge of the fact that his was a fruitful ministry made him teach and preach even more vigorously, and sent him out far from Grand Rapids with the message of redeeming grace and the returning Redeemer.

Dr. DeHaan and Yutaka Akichika, who was converted un[der] DeHaan's ministry, and is now a pastor in Jap[an]

10 Preaching . . . and teaching those things which concern the Lord Jesus Christ, with all confidence. . . . *Acts 28:31*

The Substitute

Despite the fact he preached to millions around the world by radio and did considerable traveling to speak in churches and Bible conference centers, Martin DeHaan said on numerous occasions, "I'm just a poor substitute for my brother John, who was drowned before he could become a minister."

If it's true, as some commentators believe, that Hebrews 12:1 speaks of an unseen cloud of witnesses observing the believer in action, then John DeHaan undoubtedly pressed to the front to watch and applaud his brother. He likely got even more pleasure watching Martin preach from a pulpit than when he loosened his tie, removed his jacket, and taught the Radio Bible Class before a radio microphone.

Something about being before a visible audience especially stimulated M. R. He identified with those before him, compassion gripping him. As on the radio, he spoke with unction and authority; and his rumbling voice gave audiences the feeling they were listening to a prophet.

Seldom one to harp on fringe issues, he spoke in church services and conferences more concerning the do's of the Christian life than the don'ts, preaching that when believers let the Lord Jesus live His life through them bad habits and sins of life fall away.

To DeHaan unbelief was the major issue. In his audiences he saw people playing church, needing to study the Bible and believe God's promises for them, to become mighty spiritual forces in their communities. He also saw men and women on the broad road to destruction, people desperately in need of the Savior.

In services Dr. DeHaan squirmed through what he called "interminable preliminaries." He knew that certain things had to happen before he could preach, so he tolerated congregational singing, special numbers, and announcements up to a certain point. A half-hour of preliminaries seemed sufficient: longer ones brought on the ants.

When introduced, he brushed off praise, appearing to despise it. In his opening remarks, he enjoyed ribbing fellow ministers and often included other bits of humor, bringing laughter and relaxing his audience. Then suddenly he plunged into his message in all seriousness. Much like a mighty steam locomotive thundering relentlessly across country, he rumbled along for at least forty minutes, staying on track for the Lord. Cleverly, he worked in occasional illustrations, sometimes personal ones relating to his medical days or to the out-of-doors.

In his early years of preaching, he prepared complete sermon manuscripts. By the midpoint of his career, he depended on one-page outlines. But in later years he used no notes at all, except for comments scrawled in the margins of his Bible. His prodigious mind, with its photographic memory and ability to produce information on a myriad of subjects, stood him in good stead. He was firm and organized in his thinking. One, two, three. People understood what he meant. He was easy to follow.

With great insight into the truths of the Bible, he sought to stimulate listeners to get into the Scriptures, to think and meditate on God's Word. One of his specialities was typology. In scores of Old Testament passages he found pictures of the Savior. For example, he saw Joseph, not recognized by his brothers until his second appearance to them, as a type of Christ, who came to His own and was not received but will be recognized when they see Him again.

Though he once moved about the platform gesticulating vigorously, DeHaan, conditioned by radio speaking, remained close to the pulpit during most of his preaching years and used fewer gestures. Typically he held his Bible in one hand and gestured authoratively with it, sometimes emphatically thumping the pulpit.

One of his favorite stories concerned the preacher who had only two gestures. To emphasize a point, he shook his index finger toward the ceiling, then he shook it toward the floor. This worked rather well until the day he ended a message with great emotion, saying, "When the roll is called up yonder (he vigorously pointed to the ceiling), I'll be there!" (with even greater vigor, he pointed to the floor).

The Doctor had numerous other lighter-moment stories he shared behind the scenes, with employees and others, but humor left him completely the day in the 1940s he arrived in a Western city to speak at a youth meeting and discovered he was scheduled to share the platform with a gospel horse. This beast, he learned, was so smart it could answer such a question as, "How many Persons in the Trinity?" by tapping three times. DeHaan reddened and threatened to turn the entire program over to the horse. It was either him or the steed. He wanted nothing to do with a gimmick in preaching the Word. As the story goes, the educated horse munched hay in his trailer while DeHaan vigorously preached the

Gospel, free from equestrian distractions and barnlike smells!

Young people, as well as seasoned Bible students, listened intently to DeHaan's profound but easy-to-grasp messages, and, though he didn't wear blinking bow ties or try to speak their lingo, teenagers enjoyed talking personally with him and found him a warm person. He spoke many times at Hampden Du Bose Academy in Zellwood, Florida, as well as at other schools, and after services students flocked around him, his bald head shining among them.

In Bible conferences, where he specialized in messages on prophecy and the Holy Spirit, adults pushed forward to talk to him after services. Though sometimes exhausted, having preached his heart out, he patiently chatted with admirers, answering numerous worthwhile questions and others not so relevant. One little woman tested his patience by continuing to talk on and on while others waited to greet him. Finally, as only he could do, DeHaan said, "Lady, question time is over," and he turned to talk with someone else.

Because of his familiarity with Scripture, Dr. DeHaan could fashion a sermon to suit the occasion on short notice. Arriving in Harrisburg, Pennsylvania, for a Bible conference, he learned that his hosts had been upset by a report that he had died. Someone had produced a newspaper clipping from a Michigan paper that caused the concern. The reason for the confusion was the death of another Grand Rapids DeHaan. A curious crowd assembled for the conference, and mouths dropped open as the Doctor announced his text: "Revelation 1:18 — 'I am he that liveth, and was dead; and, behold, I am alive for evermore. . . .'" He began, "The reports you heard about my death were true; I did die, but I am now here risen from the dead, and am alive forevermore."

His explanation put his audience at ease. Revelation 1:18, he said, applies first of all to the Lord Jesus Christ but also to every Christian, who was once dead in sins (Ephesians 2:1), but through the power of Christ arose (Ephesians 2:5). "Every Christian can say, 'I am one who lives in Christ. I have been crucified with Christ; nevertheless I live' (Galatians 2:20). Yes," he continued, "the report you heard was true, for I died, but now am alive forevermore! Praise the Lord!"

Dr. DeHaan's speaking engagements often took him on extensive trips. Usually his wife Priscilla accompanied him, serving as chief suitcase packer and navigator with a road map.

Curiously, Dr. DeHaan, though an authority on details relating to Israel, never journeyed to the Holy Land. Half humorously, half seriously he said, "All you do when you come back is show a lot of pictures, and you don't have time for your message." He didn't knock his close friends and others who took groups to Bible lands. That was their business. He was content to travel in the U.S. and Canada. Once Mrs. DeHaan begged him to take her across the border into Mexico when they were in California. After they spent the night in a third-rate hotel in Mexicali, Priscilla did a bit of shopping next morning as the Doctor reluctantly waited. His countenance brightened as later they crossed back to native soil.

In his travels, DeHaan had countless memorable adventures, exploring old houses, meeting and chatting with everyday sort of people, running across Radio Bible Class members in unlikely places.

Figuratively, and sometimes literally, DeHaan came to a screeching stop when he spotted a dilapidated, abandoned house, somewhat to the annoyance of Priscilla. To her it meant either a long wait in the car or a walk through musty rooms, up and down creaking stairways, poking into rat-infested basements. But to M. R. an old house brought a tingle to his spine and set his mind racing in speculative thought.

With a faraway look in his eyes, he could sit on a dusty bench and hear voices from the past. He could see and hear a young couple as they enjoyed the house after it was first built. Then there would be the gurgle of a baby's voice, the patter of small feet on the bedroom floor upstairs. The child would grow up and there would be the sad good-by as he left home. The explorer would hear the shuffling of aged feet, and then — silence. "The roof begins to leak, the floor sags, the windows are broken, the chimney begins to crumble, and now — just an abandoned house with memories," he once penned after exploring a tumbledown dwelling. And then the application: "The old crumbling shack is not the end of the story — the occupants live on — somewhere; but the question echos — *where?* Yes, the dust shall return to the earth — the hut decays — but the *spirit,* where has it gone? . . . Build your home where decay never comes and moth and rust do not corrupt!"

Though no civil rights campaigner, Dr. DeHaan was a man with a warm heart for the black man. He occasionally went out of his way to chat with Negroes on trips to the South. He got a sermon idea from a conversation with one, well up in years, seated on the stoop of his one-room shack in Mt. Dora, Florida. The aged man sat reading his Bible, at the moment seemingly unmindful of lack of panes or screens on the two windows and the door off its hinges. DeHaan stopped his car, got out and asked, "What are you reading?"

"The Good Book."

"What are you reading in the Good Book?"

"I'm reading about my new house that God is building for me in Heaven. He's preparing me a mansion in the New Jerusalem." He stopped, his hand on his well-worn Bible. "Sir, it's going to be wonderful. I don't mind a few years in this shack, for they're building me a mansion over there."

Grateful for the lesson he had learned, DeHaan gave the man a copy of *Our Daily Bread* and continued on his way.

In a Florida resort restaurant where he and Priscilla stopped one morning for breakfast, he struck up a conversation with the Negro waiter. Looking at DeHaan closely, he asked, "Are you a preacher?"

"Yes."

"A radio preacher? From Grand Rapids?"

The waiter beamed when the identity had been established. "I never knew I would meet you, Dr. DeHaan," he said. "Our whole family — and the whole neighborhood — hear you." Then he added: "The cook here in the kitchen was saved listening to the radio, and you must meet her." Soon not only the cook had come to meet the DeHaans, but news spread among other kitchen help and yard workers, and some 15 or 20 people gathered around. To DeHaan, it was another bit of evidence that his voice was familiar to many blacks, in the Southland and elsewhere.

DeHaan got further assurance that he had warm friends among Negroes when he preached in a church in Boston. Afterward, as he and Mrs. DeHaan were greeting members of the congregation, a Negro couple introduced themselves. The man was totally blind. As he took the visiting preacher's hand, he raised his sightless eyes to DeHaan's. "Dr. DeHaan, I owe my life twice to you. You were the means by God's hand of saving my life both physically and spiritually. Two years ago I was at the end of my rope completely, hopeless and despairing. It was Sunday morning, and I was planning to end it all and have it over with, as there was no use going on. As I walked across the room toward the window determined to commit suicide, I heard you preaching on the radio, and just at that moment you said something which arrested my attention. I don't remember what you said, but it struck me, and as I stopped and listened to the rest of the message I heard the plan of salvation, with the result that at the close of your sermon I accepted the invitation to receive Christ and was not only spared from bodily suicide but spiritual as well." He tightened his grip on DeHaan's hand and concluded, "Thank the Lord for the Radio Bible Class."

Many were the surprises and shattered mental pictures when Class members met or observed Dr. DeHaan for the first time. That he wore no halo and could appear and be so human encouraged some and ruffled others. At Bible conference centers, early risers were likely to meet him dressed casually, fishing rod and tackle box in hand, heading for a nearby lake. His ability always to be himself, however, had a great effect on most. At a conference center DeHaan was featured with a famous youth evangelist. "Dr. DeHaan is one of the great men of God of our day," the evangelist told his wife before they arrived, and she was somewhat edgy about meeting him. As they walked into the dining room the first day, the evangelist nudged his wife. "There is DeHaan over there." Following his gaze, she tensed, then suddenly relaxed. The famous preacher was chomping away, enjoying his meal, pushing peas onto his knife at that moment.

In other ways M. R. DeHaan proved himself not a great deal different from many other men. He had to work at being a good father and husband. And he spent some of his happiest hours of life dressed in old clothes shoveling manure from his barn and working among the vegetables in his well-tended garden.

A fishing companion, Mr. Asp, and Dr. DeHaan

The house on Leonard St.
where the DeHaans lived for many years.

11   Abide in me, and I in you. As the branch can-
      not bear fruit of itself, except it abide in the
      vine, no more can ye, except ye abide in me.
                                            John 15:4

The Farmer of Leonard Street

Those who listened closely over the years to M. R. DeHaan, and read his writings, especially his meditations in *Our Daily Bread*, sensed it: he was a farmer at heart. In 1931, shortly after he assumed the pastorate of Calvary Undenominational Church, he moved into a two-story white frame house on Leonard Street on the edge of northwest Grand Rapids. It was springtime when the DeHaans moved, and gaudy daffodils, gaily colored tulips, and sunny crocuses greeted them. Young elms that had just donned their new green finery spoke of comfortable, restful days ahead for those who would enjoy their shade, but out back of the house eleven rolling acres of land challenged the Doctor's green thumb and his outdoor spirit.

Here, at 2515 Leonard Street, the pastor and teacher, with his wife Priscilla, lived for 34 years. For the most part they were satisfying years. Here, when he could be home, he relished putting on old clothes and wearing a battered hat to do chores about the barn or to cultivate his vegetable garden. And it was here that he enjoyed the lively years that saw the four DeHaan children grow up.

When the DeHaans came to Leonard Street, Marv was five and looking forward to first grade. Ruth was 15, and, of course, in high school. June was 12, anxious for the day when she would be in school with Ruth, and Richard was a mischievous eight.

With Dad often away from home, Priscilla had the task usually of maintaining law and order. But if the Doctor was around he didn't hesitate removing his belt and taking a few whacks for misbehavior. Ruth remembers an incident or two involving her, and June recalls a "severe spanking, I think with a razor strap."

June Boone remembers her father as a man who meant what he said. "His whole personality was that way — he always did what he said he was going to do," she says.

Naturally, strong father figure that he was, DeHaan stood for no foolishness among his offspring. Take meals, for example. Despite pangs of hunger, youngsters were expected to sit reverently through a rather lengthy blessing uttered fervently by their pastor-father. After dinner, with appetites satisfied and the young children anxious to return to their activities, the family obediently sat through a devotional time. This usually consisted of Dad's reading Scripture and praying, though other family members also sometimes participated. Generally, as the children grew older, they appreciated these times together, but if anyone didn't, he dared not show it when Dad was in charge. Things were more informal when he was away. Not that anyone was bad — the youngsters were too well bred for that. But occasionally at devotional time matters got out of hand a bit. Perhaps young Marv would begin to giggle, then June would catch it, until everyone had the giggles, including Priscilla. Though not a recommended pattern, such times proved relaxing.

No doubt the fact their father was a physician as well as a minister made the DeHaan children think of him as an extra special person. He never overdoctored them, however, treating the usual illnesses quite casually sometimes to the distress of Priscilla. He prescribed aspirins for colds and other minor ailments, taking the attitude that these illnesses had to run their courses.

Dr. DeHaan set several broken bones as the children suffered growing-up spills. June broke an arm while roller skating when her father was in seminary and practicing medicine in Holland. Priscilla called him and he was there within minutes. Taking a careful, compassionate look, he had the remedy: "I'll give you 50 cents if you don't cry while I set it." His touch was gentle, and moments later the ordeal was over, and June was a half dollar richer and proud possessor of an arm cast. Once Marvin turned up with a broken arm at Gull Lake just before his father was to speak at a Bible conference gathering. Working quickly, DeHaan calmly set it. Minutes later he was preaching, seeking to minister to conferees with broken lives and spirits.

His love and compassion toward other people made a lasting impression on the children. June remembers especially the family with the mother who was mentally and physically deficient, unable properly to care for her nine children. "Dad felt very strongly for these children," June recalls. "Every autumn he outfitted them in shoes and rubbers and this sort of thing."

The children observed their father's willingness to talk to people day or night about spiritual and human problems. Once the children were hustled out of the room when a couple came to the DeHaan home seeking help. As they learned later, the man had a revolver and was threatening his wife's life. The Doctor, through wise counsel, managed

121

to convince them that God could heal their differences if they would trust Him. They did so, and the husband gave DeHaan the revolver.

Holiday times are remembered by the DeHaan children for various reasons. Dad set the tone for Thanksgiving, perhaps the most festive occasion of the year in the home, with a big turkey and all the savory trimmings. It was a time of merriment and giving of thanks to God, led by M. R. at the head of the table. Christmas was a warm, happy time, too, though Dad had deep convictions concerning what he felt was the commemoration of "a day instead of the Man, Christ Jesus." He and Priscilla agreed on a modest, Santa Clausless observance, as he faced the fact that Christmas was "here to stay — till Jesus comes to put an end to Christmas."

Without doubt the warm heart their father had toward the Word of God made a tremendous impact on the four DeHaan children. Richard trusted Christ when he was about ten years of age. "We had a good Sunday school teacher and I was really convicted one Sunday morning," he recalls. "I went home, got down on my knees, and accepted Christ as my Savior. But I know the preaching I heard Sunday after Sunday from Dad had made its impact upon me." Richard's conversion had some influence on Marv, who when he was about seven came to Christ following a Sunday service conducted by his father in Calvary Undenominational Church. June trusted Christ when she was eight in a Sunday evening service in Calvary Reformed Church, and Ruth committed her life to the Savior under her father's ministry when she was 11, also in Calvary Reformed Church.

In addition to communicating especially well to his children in regard to spiritual matters, the Doctor was a master in other areas also. Ruth, for example, remembers times when he would take her out on nature walks and point out various spring flowers, calling them all by name. There were times when he would excitedly get everyone out of bed to show them the northern lights or to watch a storm. That's the big reason Ruth says she has never been afraid of storms.

"He would sometimes take us out on the back porch during a severe electrical storm and exclaim, 'Isn't this beautiful! My Father is making it all!' " says Ruth.

He took the family on rides over the worst back roads and the ricketiest bridges he could find. He enjoyed pointing out wonders of nature as they bounced along. Because of his vast knowledge of a myriad of subjects, he stimulated the children to broaden their minds. Conversations on these back-road trips, and at home, were extremely lively, sometimes to the point of sounding like a family quarrel as they exchanged information and ideas.

Living as they did on their father's little farm, the DeHaan children not only benefited from the fresh vegetables, fruit, milk, eggs, honey, and other products, but their minds became repositories for bits of information on the best methods of operating a farm. They probably wouldn't have had a more informed tutor had they gone to agricultural school. They learned firsthand the need for pruning grapevines, for removing the suckers from below the graft on pear trees. They learned that asparagus loves salt and thrives on it, but that salt is death to weeds, as they watched Dad spread generous amounts of salt evenly over the asparagus plot in early spring.

Marv and Richard learned a memorable lesson — and a painful one for Richard — the day they accompanied Dad in the field among his beehives. One of the bees zeroed in on Richard, and, before he knew it, stung him just above the eye. He hit at it and threw himself in the grass, kicking and screaming. No sooner had the bee been brushed away than it went straight for Marv and began buzzing around his head while he, too, hid his head in the grass, screaming and calling for help.

Dad, the beekeeper, thoroughly schooled in the habits of bees from considerable reading and observation, picked Marv up and told him to stop crying. "The bee is harmless. It cannot hurt you. It has lost its sting," he said. He took him over to his elder brother, showed him the little black stinger in his brother's brow, and then said, "When the bee leaves its stinger in the victim, from then on it is perfectly harmless. The bee can still buzz and scare you, but it is powerless to hurt you. Your brother took the sting away by being stung." Then, unable to resist a sermon, he explained 1 Corinthians 15:55, "O death, where is thy sting? O grave, where is thy victory?" The Lord Jesus, "our elder Brother," hung on the cross and took the sting out of death, namely sin, and death, which has only one sting, can no longer hurt us, he explained in some detail.

The Doctor was a lover of animals, this interest adding considerably to the good times the family had together. Mike, a bulldog, was his constant companion at home for sixteen years. Mike — a short form of Microbe "because he was so small" when he was given to the family — cleared the farm of woodchucks and rats. At one stage the family had a pet sheep and a raccoon that would get peanuts out of the Doctor's pockets, but the most memorable pets were the crows Dad brought in on separate occasions. He got one of the miserable pets from a nest in the woods and for a time kept it in a box by the kitchen stove until it grew feathers. After learning to fly, it would steal clothespins from the line and send garments fluttering to the ground. When June went out to pick strawberries, the mischievous crow chased her in the house on more than one occasion. Another DeHaan crow stole a neighbor's pork chops from her kitchen table, threatening a warm friendship that existed between the two families.

The Doctor showed unusual understanding of youthful problems. As the children became old enough for a driver's license, he was generous with the family car, letting the boys use it on dates. Marv wrecked Dad's car one day, but his father had no harsh words for him, this time, nor on two or three other occasions when he came home with dented fenders. June remembers getting two speeding tickets "at the top of the hill by the cemetery, both within a few weeks of each other." As strict a disciplinarian as he was, Dad realized that she was completely shook and there was no stinging reprimand. "I always think of the verse in James, 'The Lord upbraideth not.' Dad was that way. He never rubbed it in afterward," June says.

But DeHaan was not as understanding when Marv went away to college and his senior year insisted on buying an "old klunker" from his cousin. A college boy had no business with a car, Dad told Marv in clear terms. Later, when Marv fell in love with chic Marilyn Johnson while he was in Chicago Medical School, Dr. DeHaan had some strong father-to-son advice. "Take it easy," he urged. "Before you marry, wait until you're through med school and ready to go into practice." *Like I did,* he could have added. But boys will be boys, and Marv married his last year in med school, with Dr. M. R. DeHaan officiating.

It was a source of satisfaction to the Doctor that he not only delivered all four of his children at birth but that he tied the matrimonial knots for them. Even though he wanted his sons and daughters to marry Christians, which each did, he never tried to choose mates for any of them. He put at least one to the test to determine how strong he was in the faith. Tony Haaksma, who at seventeen had trusted Christ under DeHaan's ministry, was asked to say the blessing the first time he came to dinner at Ruth's invitation. It was with much difficulty that he prayed in the presence of the Doctor. Embarrassed as he had been, he returned regularly. After his marriage to Ruth, he and the Doctor became warm companions, talking easily with one another, and fishing together often. Much the same relationship existed between the Doctor and June's husband, Rich Boone. Occasionally Marv and Richard accompanied their father on fishing trips. Today they wish these get-togethers could have been more frequent.

DeHaan was proud of his family. It warmed his heart that Marvin chose medicine, though it distressed him to some degree that, following an arm injury in mid-1960, Marvin quit surgery, returned to school, and later became a practicing psychiatrist. It also pleased him that he had not just two nurses but three in the family — besides Ruth and June, Marge, Richard's wife.

For the first years of their married lives, Richard and Ruth and their families lived near the DeHaans on Leonard Street. When grandchildren began to arrive, the grandfather bounced them on his knee till they were old enough to accompany him on trips to the barn and help him pick beans, tomatoes, strawberries, corn, and the like.

In all, DeHaan ultimately had twelve grandsons — "the Twelve Apostles," he called them. On September 5, 1960, the Marvin DeHaans added the thirteenth grandchild, a girl.

In no sense was DeHaan a doting grandfather, as much as he loved his grandchildren and despite the fact he often had a movie camera aimed at them. If he felt they weren't being disciplined properly he said so. He never showered them with gifts but rather with knowledge of God and His marvelous world. Of course, those who profited most were those who lived nearby. David Haaksma, the eldest grandchild, grew up on the Leonard Street farm at Grandpa's heels. (Later, after going to work for the Radio Bible Class in its book department, he took over the DeHaan garden when his grandfather's health began to fail.) He'll always remember Grandpa's calm reaction when his palomino mare was giving birth to a colt. David burst into the DeHaan kitchen, shouting the news. "I have to call the veterinarian! Penny is having a baby!" M. R. quieted David with the assurance it was quite a natural process; and with a little assistance from Grandfather, Penny gave birth to a splendid mare colt. David watched with delight as thirty minutes later she struggled to her feet and "went straight to the 'cafeteria,'" as DeHaan once described it, "and soon was 'gurgling' and nursing to her heart's content."

Even the grandchildren who lived away from Grand Rapids saw Grandfather often enough to have him make an impact on them. Jon and Rick Boone are examples. When fishing with Grandpa, Jon would row the boat and at the same time learn lessons from him concerning the habits of fish. Rick enjoyed the automobile rides and other activities during which his grandfather would teach him to recognize the different trees and various animals. By his mid-teens, Rick had become such an animal lover that he had a home zoo, including rats, turtles, and snakes.

Without doubt the most important human element in the life of M. R. DeHaan was Priscilla. Calm, steady, even-tempered, she was the balance wheel to keep the sometimes high, sometimes low Doctor ticking just right. For him there seemed to be no medium mood as he kept up with the tremendous load of work that he carried. Never a nagger, Mother, as he usually called Priscilla, had just the right word, the right touch, the right look, and knew how to handle delicate situations.

When he was going through rough days in both Calvary churches, Priscilla quieted him, encouraged, prayed with him. She answered anonymous phone calls, sometimes listening to mean digs meant for him. Priscilla wished to protect her husband if possible.

In matters of food, she knew what to cook to please him, though actually his was no finicky appetite. He was mainly a meats-and-vegetables man, occasionally enjoyed potatoes with lots of salt, and had a taste for certain spicy dishes. Pea soup was his favorite and he could make a meal on a large bowlful. He didn't care a lot about desserts, though she knew she could delight him with peaches and cream.

It was Priscilla who helped keep M. R. dressed neatly — except when he was home wearing his gardening clothes. He might have showed up at Radio Bible Class with rumpled trousers and unshined shoes — but Priscilla made it impossible. She not only pressed his trousers but kept his shoes polished. Besides all this, she patiently sat by as he carried on his work in his study into the night hours.

Though M. R. was a man who enjoyed talking to people,

he usually tagged along reluctantly with Priscilla to social gatherings. But he especially enjoyed one group made up of several couples from Calvary Undenominational Church days who for many years gathered for anniversaries and the like. In practically all social affairs DeHaan generally dominated conversations, usually turning discussions to matters relating to Scripture. In a sense, the party would end up as a two-hour Bible lesson, probably on world conditions and prophecy. If this didn't happen and the conversation degenerated to chit-chat, the Doctor preferred to drop into a comfortable chair and sleep. But even in these instances Priscilla showed understanding, calmly accepting it as part of the makeup of the man she married.

M. R. occasionally enjoyed referring to Priscilla in sermon illustrations. He claimed he never really understood his wife. "This vase must stand exactly here, and that figurine must be there — not an inch either way," he once wrote. "The salad must sleep on a bed of rabbit food — lettuce, water cress, or some other cattle feed. The meat must be decorated with parsley. The cherry on the dessert must rest right on top of the pudding. Yes, women are different, and how glad I am. What a drab world it would be if they had no more sense of beauty, adornment, and artistic arrangement than we men. And so while we don't understand them, we *appreciate* them."

Once he humorously claimed he had been married to six different wives, and was then living with his seventh. Quickly he explained that "science tells us that we get a new body every seven years. The cells of our bodies are used up in the process of metabolism, and there is a complete change of tissue every seven years. But the soul and spirit remain the same. Though the house changes, the occupant remains the same. Therefore, in our 44 years of married life, I've had six wives but in reality the same wife, a *wonderful* one!"

Being the high-low man that he was, M. R. did not always treat Priscilla like the queen he really considered her to be. On one occasion the Holy Spirit convicted him through a meditation he himself had written. Arriving at the office one morning, he told the story:

"This morning Mrs. DeHaan and I had a little disagreement, and I didn't say anything at all as we ate breakfast. Finally it was time to read the devotional in *Our Daily Bread*. She did so silently to herself for a moment. Then taking it and shoving it under my nose she asked, 'Are you the man who wrote this?' I read the article and felt about an inch tall. It had to do with kindness and forbearance. That did it. We had to make up right there. It's so easy to preach but so much more difficult to practice."

Saint that he was, and Bible teacher supreme, M. R. DeHaan reckoned himself human. And because he was thoroughly human — and a lover of not only the Word but the magnificent world that God gave mankind — he lived for the times he and Priscilla could journey to a secluded spot called "Rest-a-While" in Northern Wisconsin and be alone in a vast unspoiled forest to write and relax — and fish — in a shimmering lake and gurgling trout streams.

A well-known photo of Dr. DeHaan, used on his books
and in Radio Bible Class materials.

The Carlson cabin, "Rest-a-while," in the north woods.

"Happiness is in a fishing boat."

12

God's best school has horizons for walls, a sky for a roof, and the earth for its floor.

M. R. DeHaan

"Rest-a-While"

Apart from his Bible and family, M. R. DeHaan, as indicated by his gardening, liked nothing better in life than to drink deeply from the world that his Heavenly Father had so magnificently fashioned. Even while he worked in his study at home, sights and sounds of nature interrupted him and put him in a trance at his window: a robin on her nest calmly riding out a fierce storm . . . a wise little chipmunk looking like a boy with double mumps as he scampered about on a bright fall day storing food for the winter months ahead . . . brash crows taunting a stolid gray owl . . . a choir of birds lustily singing after a spring shower . . . a well-camouflaged tree frog playing hide-and-seek and serenading from a nearby elm. These and a thousand more sights and sounds held the Doctor spellbound and often colorfully enlivened his devotional meditations.

While he enjoyed hunting, until he gave it up for health reasons, DeHaan rated fishing as his number one outdoor interest. This adventurous sport took him over the years into trout streams in Michigan, Wisconsin, Kentucky, the Colorado Rockies, and Canada, into Puget Sound, waters off the Florida coast, and bass lakes elsewhere. From an outdoor viewpoint, he was never happier than when he had a fly-rod in his hand and a fishing buddy at his side — a grandson, a son or son-in-law, or sidekicks such as Frank O'Dell and Jake De Vogel, men of a similar stocky build whose rugged personalities dovetailed perfectly with DeHaan's.

It was in the summer of 1945, on a visit to Norway, in upper Michigan, to fish with another friend, Dad Asp, and preach in a small church in the area, that DeHaan was introduced to a place he came to love more than any other spot in the vast outdoor wonderland — and to two people who were to become part of his inner circle of friends. Mrs. Clarence Carlson, whose heart hungered for a firmer grasp of the truths of God's Word, drove twelve miles to Norway from Iron Mountain to hear DeHaan preach. Afterward she greeted him and, mentioning that she heard of his interest in fishing, half jestingly invited him to the cottage she and her husband owned on a good fishing lake just over the border from Iron Mountain in Wisconsin. To her surprise, M. R. took her up on the offer, coming with Priscilla to their cottage a few weeks later.

Nestled in a vast virgin forest high above Patton* Lake, the cottage, appropriately named "Rest-a-While," captured DeHaan's heart from the beginning. Its primitiveness made him feel like a pioneer: a hard-to-operate pump out front, a woodstove, gas light in the living room and kerosene lamps
*Also spelled Patten.

in other rooms, a dilapidated dock, and an old-fashioned outhouse painted green.

In the mid-50's the Carlsons modernized "Rest-a-While," putting in electricity, running water, toilet facilities, and adding rooms, including a dining room overlooking the lake, and a new dock. The upstairs was made into three rooms, and one room was set aside especially for the DeHaans. At the entrance to the room Clarence Carlson put a bearskin rug, and his wife Rachel selected blue and white striped curtains and a matching counterpane for the bed to blend with the blue walls.

To the Carlsons, this was M. R. DeHaan's cottage. He was given everything but the deed, as he and Priscilla and various other members of the family visited "Rest-a-While" spring and fall year after year. He tried to dissuade Clarence and Rachel from modernizing, but he adjusted himself to appreciate everything — from the instant heat to the modern kitchen where he brewed coffee before going on the lake for a morning's catch.

In the Carlsons' mind, "Rest-a-While" was sort of a big prophet's chamber, where the man they came to love so deeply could come and unwind, away from the phone and office work, and be completely himself while he fished, wrote, and feasted on the sights about him. From his chair at one end of the long birch table in the knotty pine dining room, where he scrawled countless manuscript pages of meditations and books, he saw through the picture window with its eastern exposure a constantly changing breath-taking scene that quickened his pulse and pen. As the sun rose, the lake became a gray-blue mirror, until a breeze began to play upon it, turning it to shimmering diamonds. Crisp autumn mornings unfurled azure skies that accented colorful foliage along the shoreline — exciting crimsons and scarlets of the sumac and red maples, luscious yellows of the birches, quaking aspens, and sugar maples, and dark greens of towering pyramidlike white spruces, hemlocks, and pines. In afternoons, likely as not, fleecy clouds would begin a swift, endless parade of changing shapes from the west.

"My Father painted it all!" the entranced Doctor said time and again.

Once, after a fruitless period of fishing on the lake, DeHaan sat at the dining table in his favorite big black chair and studied a great blue heron standing in the shallow water as motionless as a statue. He was moved to describe the lesson he learned from the heron:

"His long neck with the javelin at the end was poised for action, but not a move. One might think he was dead except that he was standing up. Five minutes passed and still no action, and then quietly, imperceptibly he raised one long leg slowly — oh, so slowly — and then the other without disturbing the water in the least. And then, straight for the mark, the beak descended upon the hapless perch. Flying with his catch to the bank, he had his dinner. . . . I had been a failure as a fisherman, and now I know why. First, I didn't have the patience of a blue heron. I gave up too quickly. Next, I didn't keep myself unnoticed like that statuesque bird. . . ."

On the lake itself, rowing his stubby brown boat or chuging along in it powered by his three-horse Evinrude, the Doctor drank in the glories of the unspoiled wilderness. Fishing was forgotten once as he watched a bald eagle, huge wings outstretched and motionless, its white head and tail gleaming in the morning sun, wheel and glide to the edge of the lake and pick up a fish. Then, wings flapping powerfully, it lighted on a dead tree to quickly gulp its breakfast, before spiraling upward and disappearing in the blue. Or if it was autumn, the fisherman might see a flock of geese drop down in north bay and cross the lake, and quietly position himself to observe them.

He was intrigued by the four-footed wildlife and slithering reptiles of the forest, and to see them he enjoyed leisurely drives over narrow roads that tunneled through the towering trees. Up ahead he would sometimes see skittish deer beside the road that dashed into the forest as his car approached. A red streak crossed and he knew it was a red fox. Farther on a black bear nibbled blueberries in a clearing, and a three-foot pine snake wriggled its way from the undergrowth.

In the north woods, particularly on moonless nights, myriads of stars spangle the pitch black sky. Once DeHaan penned his feelings: "I have just come in from outdoors and I am dizzy and amazed. With my field glasses I swept the heavens and came to a new appreciation of the words of David, 'When I consider Thy heavens . . . what is man . . . ?' (Psalm 8:3, 4)."

Everywhere he looked, the teacher of the Radio Bible Class saw hidden Bible truths. "He could look at anything in nature and come up with a story that had to do with redemption," recalls Clarence Carlson. "Whether it was fish, a tree, or an animal, he could see the handwriting of God and its relationship to the Word of God. Take the lake, for example. He talked about how it sustained life and how it could also take life. It would hold you up but it could also take your life if you were not in a boat. So, as he pointed out, the Word of God has the power, too, to take your life or to sustain your life. If you didn't drink water, you would die — and he'd drink water right out of his hat! This was true of God's Word — you had to drink it to live."

As the years passed, DeHaan and Carlson — a soft-spoken, perceptive man about ten years DeHaan's junior — became the warmest of friends. They fished together and shared thoughts from the Bible, with Clarence generally on the receiving end. Manufacturer of about 80 per cent of the wooden handles and backing of rubber stamps used in the United States, Carlson describes himself as a rather wobbly Christian until he encountered DeHaan.

"After I got to know the truth of the grace of God, I started to teach Sunday school," says Carlson. "I grew in the knowledge of the Word so that after a while I was able to study by myself. Sometimes I'd come out to the cottage and he'd go over a chapter for me verse by verse, pointing out details and outlines that I could bring out to my Sunday school class. He'd sit here for hours and just talk to me. If he wasn't in the area, I'd call him long distance to talk over some point of Scripture. The Doctor gave me a message. He taught me what it means to be justified by faith. And the second coming and the righteousness of God he just opened up in a marvelous way."

Mrs. Carlson tells a similar story, growing considerably in her spiritual life and becoming a person capable of teaching others as a result of her contact with Dr. DeHaan. The Carlsons would drop in on the DeHaans on a warm evening and find him stripped to the waist and barefoot, resting in the living room with Mrs. DeHaan. After dressing, including white shirt and tie, he would teach the Carlsons from the Bible as if they were a large audience.

Clarence Carlson still remembers the day he finally began to rethink his position on eternal security. He frankly told DeHaan he believed a Christian could "fall from grace" through sinning. "The Doctor took hold of me and marched me behind the cottage here and just about shook the daylights out of me. He looked me square in the eye and said: 'Clarence, if it isn't *all of grace*, we're all sunk!' It convinced me so much that I started to study and it wasn't too long before I really had my eyes open to this marvelous truth of the security of the believer in Christ."

The Carlsons assert that much of the fundamental Bible teaching in the Iron Mountain area grew out of Dr. DeHaan's visits. At the cottage he conducted Bible studies for friends the Carlsons invited in. He preached in small country churches to congregations of 30 or 40 on many occasions. He talked to the residents and vacationers at the lake, knowing many personally and sharing with them the Gospel.

Once he preached to a barbershopful of men in Iron Mountain. As the Doctor sat waiting his turn, a loudmouth came in and quipped to a barber, "I've got a good bargain for you. I can get you a ticket straight through to Heaven for $25, and when you get there, if you don't like it, you can come back and I'll give you your money back and you can go to Hell."

There were a few guffaws, but not from the smoldering DeHaan. His gravel voice ground out: "I can get you a ticket straight through to Heaven for free. That price was paid by Jesus Christ on Calvary 2,000 years ago."

The loudmouth chided, "You don't believe that stuff!"

The Doctor's blood pressure rising, he cut loose with a tongue lashing that gave the man a barbershop trimming he hadn't bargained for, and he left, his neck red and hair uncut.

DeHaan dealt severely with anyone who flippantly handled God's truths. Even for Christians who misquoted Scripture he had a sharp word of reprimand.

The Doctor had countless memorable adventures fishing. As a pastor, he sometimes took youngsters to lakes outside Grand Rapids and taught them the art of plunking a lure in just the right spot. Tony Haaksma was one of the boys, fishing with the Doctor even before he was acquainted with Ruth. As a son-in-law, Tony often came to Patton Lake with the man he considered a master fisherman. He recalls:

"I learned to fly-fish from him. As I would do so, he would say, 'Try that pocket over there' — a small opening just big enough to lay a fly in. Then he would demonstrate and laying the fly smack in the center would pull out a bass. I'm sure it was a matter of luck to some extent, but he knew how to do it. And he knew where the fish might be. He always said you've got to think like a fish. You've got to know what they're looking for and give it to them."

He liked to try an occasional new lure or fishing gadget, but he never fell for what he considered pure gimmicks. There were a few times when the Doctor was wrong on some point related to fishing and admitted it. Rich Boone, a son-in-law, remembers how he was ribbed, on various occasions, when he fell for some highly advertised newfangled lure. Once as they prepared to fish on the Pine River near "Rest-a-While," the older fisherman chuckled with ridicule as Rich tied on one of the fancy spinners he had bought in Iron

Mountain. But it was a serious-faced DeHaan who, swallowing his pride, asked Rich some time later, "Say, you got another one of those things?" The Doctor had worked through his assortment of flies (kept in the band of his hat) but had caught nothing, whereas Rich had hooked six trout. The expert then tied on a spinner and within a short time they had their limit. Later, further conceding that Rich had discovered a good thing, he went into town and bought several of these lures, in varying sizes, for himself.

DeHaan had a curious mind. He investigated everything. He sounded the bottom of Patton Lake to determine depths, and through other observation he knew the mile long lake from one end to the other.

Despite the enjoyment he got from fishing and being outdoors, work was the big thing in M. R. DeHaan's life. Through radio teaching, preaching, and his writings he worked to draw the net to win men and women to the Savior. He had deep convictions about what the Gospel could do when it was cast out to the masses. He preached and taught it and at Patton Lake he wrote with even greater enthusiasm than he fished.

Dr. DeHaan in a
characteristic teaching pose.

Dr. DeHaan at
the blackboard.

Dr. De Haan at the doorway
of the modern Radio Bible Class building.

13

There is laid up . . . a crown of righteousness
. . . unto all them also that love His appearing.

2 *Timothy 4:8*

Perhaps Today

The man stood in the grove of hemlocks, his eyes twinkling a bit as he looked at the giant pine. He estimated that the tree measured more than fourteen feet around the base. Gazing upward, he guessed it towered at least 120 feet; in any case it dwarfed the hemlocks. The man had the same thought as he did the half dozen other times he had made pilgrimages to the giant pine. If only he had an area enclosed with small mesh netting to keep out the deer flies and mosquitoes, he could bring a table, chair, and paper and write there beneath the big pine tree. There would be no end to the inspiration he could get from such a setting.

This little dream of M. R. DeHaan's never worked out on

his visits to Patton Lake, but nevertheless he did get inspiration enough in other spots in the area to turn out reams of manuscript copy on his busman's holidays in northern Wisconsin. Once he sat on a logging bridge and penned a meditation. The singing, dancing river whispered thoughts to him — God's thoughts: "There are three stanzas to my song. The first is about my source, the second is about my journey, and the third is about my goal."

Then the writer explained: "The source is a never-failing spring deep in the hills. Isaiah tells us that 'the glorious Lord will be to us a place of broad rivers and streams' (Isaiah 33:21). The peace of God's river is not monotony but constant variety; there are rapids, runs, waterfalls, and peaceful pools. So, too, the heart at peace with God experiences all the vicissitudes of life, of weal and woe, of joy and sorrow — but — at the same time — always *peace*. The goal of the river is the ocean — even so we too must lose ourselves in the ocean of God's love, for only then will our peace know its fullness in the eternal rest. Can you imagine! I used to think a river was good only for catching fish!"

Of course, the bulk of DeHaan's writing at the lake was at one end of the long birch table in the sun-parlor-like dining room overlooking the sparkling waters. He used 8½″ x 11″ typing paper, writing in ink with a strong, steady hand, and unconcerned with margins. His style was relatively simple and down to earth, flowing smoothly, his thoughts easy to follow. Usually he was up early writing, a couple of hours ahead of Mrs. DeHaan or other members of the family who might have been along.

Back at the office, he presented his manuscript to his secretary, Lee (as he called Leona Hertel), trusting her to make minor corrections as she typed it.

When in Grand Rapids, DeHaan, of course, did much of his writing in his study at home. He used few reference books, usually the only volume open on his desk being a well-marked King James Bible. (He abhorred most of the new versions, branding them "versions and perversions.") Like other writers, he hit dry periods, and stared out the window hoping for a sudden inspiration. Once he sat there "thinking, thinking, without a worthwhile idea entering my head," he later wrote. "I was trying desperately to get an inspiration for an article for *Our Daily Bread* but nothing would come. Disappointedly, I gave up, walked outside, and stretched myself on the grass — and *looked up*. And there was my inspiration. I slipped into one of those pleasant moods of reverie, where imagination runs free and easy. I imagined those fleecy clouds were living things traversing the skies to meet for some joyous occasion. There was a fleecy cloud shaped exactly like a gamboling lamb. And there was a huge gray elephant with trunk and all. Another cloud became a giant ship loaded with people, while over in the west there were islands of sun-drenched beauty. Faces began to appear, faces of loved ones — and — then two clouds folded together, and, as the sun streaked their edges with a snow-white border of light, the face of all faces, beautiful beyond description, was formed in fleeting outline, and then the vapors tumbled apart. But I had seen a face — unlike any other. With eyes fixed upon the rift in the clouds, peering into the endless depth of blue, I visualized that day when He shall come and we shall *'see His face.'* "

DeHaan went on to say that he awakened from his reverie and realized it was "not all a dream, for *He is coming again — it could be today!*"

If any doctrine excited M. R. DeHaan above another, it was the doctrine of the second coming of Jesus Christ. From his early days as a preacher and teacher, he proclaimed the glad news of the coming again of the God-Man. One man, after hearing DeHaan preach at Moody Bible Institute's Founders Week conference, said he had heard many preachers speak about the return of the Lord. "But," he said, "they spoke about it like they were delivering a lecture. Dr. DeHaan moved me tremendously because here was a

145

man who really *believed* the Lord was coming back as a practical reality." DeHaan devoted many pages to the subject in his 25 books and numerous booklets, and wrote about it in countless devotional articles. His books giving major emphasis to the return of Christ are *The Second Coming of Jesus* (1944), *Signs of the Times* (1951), and *Coming Events in Prophecy* (1962).

In *Coming Events in Prophecy* he wrote: "As we look upon conditions in the world today, if we did not have this hope of Christ's returning, and we had to rely upon the power of the Church, and the testimony of Christians to bring about the cessation of hostilities and to bring in perfect righteousness, I for one would despair and give up hope entirely. If I did not believe in the imminent, personal return of the Lord Jesus to make right that which is all wrong in this world today, and to bring in the peace for which man has so long been sighing, and for which he has so long been looking, I don't think I would care to preach another sermon. I would have to admit that the whole thing is a failure, and that the Gospel has not accomplished that which we had expected it to do, and that Christianity is nothing else but another religion and a tremendous farce."

But pointing out that Christ's last promise to His disciples was "I am coming again" and that the last promise of the Bible is "surely I come quickly," he wrote, ". . . just as surely as Jesus came and died on the cross the first time, and arose from the grave, and ascended into Heaven, He is coming again; coming again to put a stop to all the wickedness and all the inequality and iniquity of this present day, put an end to man's rule of failure and bungling, and to set up His glorious Millennial Kingdom."

Hardly a day passed but that the Doctor made some reference to the imminent return of the Lord to one or more of his co-workers or others. He often talked about it in RBC devotional times. The thought did more to give him a good start for each day than his early morning coffee.

Some years ago an Australian listener to the Radio Bible Class broadcast sent DeHaan an attractive plaque which says, "Perhaps Today." He put it on the edge of his desk facing the door. It was the first thing DeHaan looked at as he entered his office. "It reminds me of the tremendous responsibility of this one day [I am living now], because the motto is certainly true according to the promise of the Book, *perhaps today,*" he wrote in 1964.

At the beginning of every year, DeHaan said, "I am looking for the Lord Jesus to come this year. But, if He doesn't, then I'll look for Him next year."

In no sense did DeHaan's intense interest in the second coming cause him to lay aside responsibilities and go to a hilltop to await Christ's return, as did date-setting William Miller and his followers twice in 1844. While DeHaan believed the Lord might come at any moment, he kept busy, "diligent in season, out of season," faithfully, fervently getting out the Gospel to far-flung areas.

Whatever M. R. DeHaan believed, he believed thoroughly. Once an associate asked him how he "leaned" on a certain theological question. Characteristically, he retorted: "I never like lean-to's. I'm either in one tent or another. I'm never in a lean-to." He smiled. "If I know it, I know it; if I don't, I don't."

In his last book, *Portraits of Christ in Genesis* (published in 1966 after his death), DeHaan set the record straight on several contemporary issues in their relationship to him:

"So often we become disturbed by conditions in the world, the increase in crime, violence, and wickedness, the rapid spread of Communism, the apostasy of the Church, and the threat of a great racial struggle or an atomic conflict. . . . But all these things have been foretold and are under the complete control of our God. . . . As a preacher of the Gospel, I have that one commission, 'Preach the Word,' and when I depart from this to join the forces which would bring in a man-made Great Society, I am unfaithful to my calling. It is not my business as a preacher to spend my time in civil rights demonstrations, or seeking to bring a Utopia on earth during this dispensation. My one task shall be to preach the Word, not expecting to solve the problems of the nations until Jesus comes."

14

In my Father's house are many mansions: if it were not so, I would have told you. I go to prepare a place for you. *John 14:2*

Welcome Home

When the 10 a.m. coffee break bell rang in the offices of Radio Bible Class on June 25, 1964, the approximately 80 employees laid aside their work and went downstairs to the lunchroom. Word had been circulated that everyone was expected for a special event. When all had gathered, Dr. and Mrs. DeHaan were asked to come down, the "committee" having arranged for Priscilla to be in the building that morning. When the DeHaans came in, a pianist played a few measures of the bridal march to set the atmosphere. For this was the DeHaans' Golden Wedding anniversary.

Leona Hertel, the Doctor's secretary, who had headed the group that planned the occasion, pinned a corsage on the blue dress of the attractive, smiling Priscilla, and in turn put a boutonniere on the lapel of the blue checked sports jacket of the surprised but delighted RBC teacher.

Leona had a little presentation speech prepared as she handed the DeHaans an appropriately engraved loving cup mounted on a carved teakwood base, but her words turned to tears. As one staff member said to Leona afterward, "There are occasions when tears are more eloquent than words!"

Among those planning the Golden Wedding coffee break there were gnawing thoughts that this might be the last time they could honor Dr. DeHaan in a special manner. At 73, he showed increased outward signs of failing health, though he still often revealed the bursts of energy for which he was known. Usually the first to arrive at the office, he had never limited himself to a 40-hour week, and he didn't now. He continued to tape broadcasts, and there was always writing to do, along with administrative details and speaking engagements. In carrying out his numerous duties, he exhibited the same sharpness of mind, despite his physical deterioration. In an *Our Daily Bread* item in the early '60s, he himself wrote:

"The Owner of the 'house' I have occupied here on earth has served notice that I must soon move out. He will not make many more repairs — since I am going to vacate it anyway. The foundation is crumbling, the roof leaks, the heating system is failing, and the windows are getting dim. The steps are getting shaky and the hinges are getting rusty and squeaky." Yet, as he added, he didn't dread the thought of "moving": "I have been overwhelmed by the innumerable advantages of that new Home over this old one; so much so that now instead of dreading it, I am beginning to get anxious to move. If it were not for a few things I still have to do, I would want to move pronto."

He never asked for sympathy. If someone asked how he felt, with a little smile he would answer, "You shouldn't ask me that."

150

During his declining years, the Doctor, quite aware of his history of coronaries, relied to some degree on medication to keep himself going. Once his doctor gave him a prescription, but DeHaan had already prescribed it for himself and had been "taking twice that much of the same medicine for two years," he confided to an associate.

Because of a tendency to be overweight, the Doctor tried to be moderate in his eating habits. Sometimes invitations out to dinner nullified his good intentions. "Henry, I sinned again," he once told Henry Bosch. "I ate more than I should have. But it was so delicious and they kept pushing it on me."

He continued to take his coffee hot — steaming hot — and extra strong. A cup or two helped him start the day — not as early as in his younger years, but usually not later than 6:30. Before the coffee, came a time when he talked with the Lord as he lay in bed. He put it in these words: "I have learned the value of 'staying in bed' a little while after I awaken — just to think — pray — and plan my day, all with eternity in view. A few minutes' 'seeking first' the things of God . . . in the morning, is time well spent!"

Undoubtedly his close communion with God kept the Doctor from becoming a sour, cantankerous person in his last years. Some who had locked horns with him in conferences and knew him as a man of spirit and conviction felt he mellowed as he reached his threescore and ten years. But tell him that and he'd snort, "Don't say that! I know fruit. The next thing after mellow is rotten!" With that his face would break into his half smile.

The Doctor was painfully aware of the earthen qualities of the vessel God was using. Though he believed that the atoning work of Christ made him secure in the family of God, he once lamented to a friend that he was bothered by "all the things that I'll have to account for at the judgment seat of Christ." With tears on his cheeks, he acknowledged, however, that he had come a long way: "I was born with a quick temper, and it has taken the grace of God to cool me down."

In February, 1965, Dr. DeHaan spoke at the Moody Bible Institute Founders Week conference in Chicago. He puffed his way in below-zero weather to and from Moody Church. The bitter cold, together with his climb up the stairs to his second floor room in a nearby motel, aggravated his heart condition. Though he finished his assignment in traditional style, severe chest pains made it an exhausting experience.

The Founders Week conference proved to be his last public meeting. Upon returning to Grand Rapids, he was hospitalized by his doctor for two weeks. This enforced period of rest gave him new vigor, as he resumed his duties. But soon afterward, an attack of shingles hit him. He insisted on going to the office and his secretary, Leona, scolded, "Don't you know you're supposed to be in bed resting when you have shingles?"

He peered at her from the top of his glasses, a twinkle in his eyes. "And which medical school did you get your degree from?" He continued working.

On the evening of July 29 tragedy struck. As the teacher of the Radio Bible Class and Priscilla drove north a few miles out of Grand Rapids toward Sparta, Michigan, the vehicle ahead slowed down quickly to make a right turn. The Doctor's car swerved to the left and collided head-on with a station wagon. Dr. DeHaan slammed into the windshield, breaking it. He was hospitalized with severe head lacerations, an injured left leg, and extensive damage to his breastbone and ribs. Mrs. DeHaan was treated and released, having suffered minor injuries. When news of the accident hit the press, calls poured into Grand Rapids from many parts of the United States.

The Doctor was hospitalized for almost two weeks. He bled profusely as a result of medication he had been taking to thin the blood. His face was black and blue. It was during this period that he heard a broadcast tape that brought tears to his eyes. Recorded earlier for release at that time, he heard Richard making the familiar introduction, "Now here is my father, Dr. DeHaan." The battered, heavily lined face of the patient brightened. "Just thank the Lord, Mother!" he said with great emotion to Priscilla, who sat at his bedside.

When the Doctor was released from the hospital, he was far from well. Since the accident he had been suffering a recurrence of those chest pains. But he soon pushed himself to resume broadcasting and writing. Against Priscilla's wishes, he continued to drive. One of his first outings was the office picnic, August 27, which had been scheduled for July 30 but postponed because of the accident. Bob Roush phoned from the office to tell the Doctor that someone would pick up him and Mrs. DeHaan. But the plucky Doctor snorted, "No, I'll drive myself. What do you think I am, an invalid?"

In late summer he had a hankering to go north once again to the Carlsons' "Rest-a-While" cottage. He wasn't strong enough to fish, except while sitting on the bank of a quiet stream. His son-in-law and daughter, Rich and June Boone, drove the DeHaans to the northern Wisconsin cottage, where they enjoyed a few days in this woodland setting which the Doctor loved so much. But there were lumps in throats as the DeHaans prepared to leave, for the grand old fisherman gathered his fishing gear to take back to Grand Rapids. Before, he had always left it . . .

Back home, office visits were few and far between, as Dr. DeHaan did most of his work at the house. Recording equipment had been installed in his study and here he could make tapes when he felt the strength to do so. If he did work at the office, he came home and slept all afternoon. He ate supper, then went back to bed, exhausted. Yet there was no doubt in Doctor's mind about retiring from his job. He often said, "There's no retirement for the Christian.

Don't talk about retirement. The world is too needy; we can't retire!"

A man of the Book, the Doctor spent endless hours poring over Scriptures. Thoughts of being caught up to be with the Lord quickened his pulse. It was the way he wanted to go; "perhaps today," he continued to say.

But in early December the 74-year-old DeHaan sensed that God was about to take him by way of the Valley. Long his favorite song had been, "Where the Gates Swing Outward Never," and he felt he would soon be a resident of that heavenly place. He called his three grandsons, David, Jim, and Dale Haaksma who lived nearby, and like a patriarch of old, talked and prayed for them, despite chest pains and labored breathing. Nothing would have pleased him more than to have gathered all 13 of his grandchildren, but they were scattered too far. A shining jewel to him, M. R. II, Richard's eldest, was a student in Chicago at Moody Bible Institute.

The Doctor rallied from this sinking experience, but afterward expressed some disappointment. He told a visitor, "I went through all the death agonies and I thought sure I would open my eyes and see the Lord. I'm so curious I can hardly wait. Now I'll have to go through the death struggle again."

By this time Dr. DeHaan had completed his 25th, and last, book, *Portraits of Christ in Genesis*. As his strength permitted, he worked at taping these messages in his studio at home. He expressed great concern to members of the family — and to the Lord — that the entire series be aired on the Radio Bible Class. Richard assured him that if God should call his father Home before he could do so himself, he would complete the series from the manuscript. The Doctor seemed to breathe a sigh of relief upon hearing this. It not only told him that the Genesis lessons would all be broadcast but assured him that his son Richard would be stepping into his place.

The alternately gray and bright, crisp December days passed slowly for the Doctor. Propped on a large green chair in his bedroom, his face benign and tired, he watched the ever-changing scene from his window. Ice partially covered the lake formed by the Thornapple River, and occasionally children skated near the shore, perhaps fifty yards away. Birds flitted here and there in search of food, and sometimes a rabbit hopped by, oblivious to the eyes of the pajama-clad figure watching from the bedroom. A light, wet snow during the night turned the outdoors to a lacy white wonderland accented against a blue sky swept clean of clouds by the morning sun. "My Father painted this magnificent scene," the man in the green chair would say.

On Saturday, December 11, Dr. DeHaan's physician prescribed quinine for heart palpitations, and the weary patient took a dose about 4 p.m. His son Marvin visited with him, leaving for home on Sunday. Doctor's daughter Ruth and Richard's wife Marge, both nurses, alternated in caring for Dr. DeHaan, as they had done for the past two weeks. Sunday night he suffered a severe attack, gasping for breath till his complexion seemed almost blue. Oxygen from the tank beside his bed ultimately gave him relief.

Monday morning, December 13, Ruth changed his bedding, sponged him off, and he seemed refreshed enough to attempt another Genesis tape. "Put a chair here and there from my bed to the study, and if I can't make it, I'll sit down and rest." He managed to record almost an entire message, but before its completion he weakened to the point that Ruth helped him back to bed.

That afternoon Henry Bosch and Dr. Raymond Brown from the office visited with Dr. DeHaan for a few minutes. "Why there's old Caleb!" the Doctor quipped upon seeing the aged, white-haired Dr. Brown. The Doctor was in pajamas, raised slightly in the hospital bed that had been obtained for him, his Bible and writing materials at his side. He was preparing meditations for *Our Daily Bread*.

155

To both Bosch and Brown, the Doctor seemed stronger than they had expected. Though they did most of the talking, he added gravelly bits of humor to the conversation and told of doing a partial Genesis message that morning. Bosch ended the visit with prayer, and the men returned to the office, much encouraged.

About 4:30 P.M. Dr. DeHaan asked Priscilla for his bathrobe and slippers and she helped him to the green chair beside his bed. Ruth had gone home, two doors away. Meantime, her husband Tony dropped in, and he and Doctor talked quietly, admiring the icy scene on the lake out back.

Presently, about 5:30 o'clock, the Doctor, breathing heavily, asked Tony for the oxygen mask. Before his son-in-law could turn on the oxygen, the beloved teacher gasped and was gone. He had entered the presence of the King.

As the Doctor himself had once written, nothing compares "with the homegoing of a saint of God . . . to go Home, to leave these old clods of clay, to be loosed from bondage of the material, to be set free, to say good-by to mortality, . . . welcomed by the innumerable company of angels, and then — glory, hallelujah — to be introduced to the King, and hear Him say, 'Welcome home, my child.' . . . No wonder the Bible says, 'How precious is the death of His saints'."

In the hours following her husband's death, numerous messages came to Mrs. DeHaan: "A stout oaken timber in God's forest has fallen . . ."/"For Dr. DeHaan, a higher calling. For us a great loss."/"He was beloved by all of us and will be greatly missed."/"He will be remembered over much of the world as valiant for God's truth."/"When we told our children, our eight-year-old burst into tears. That's how much Dr. DeHaan and his books and booklets and program have been a part of our lives for the past six years."

The memorial service was held in Calvary Undenominational Church. Approximately 1,500 persons came to pay tribute, including a Class member from Montana wearing dust-covered cowboy boots who told someone, "I just had to come . . . to see that man." Dr. Theodore Epp and the Rev. Herbert Vander Lugt, Dr. DeHaan's pastor, brought the messages and one of two songs sung by Clair Hess and Ray Felten was the familiar, "Tell Me the Story of Jesus."

Rain which had been falling intermittently for several days had changed to snow during the service. At the grave site Dr. Epp, his overcoat collar turned up, prayed and committed the earthly remains of the beloved teacher back to the dust. Somehow the falling snow seemed to symbolize the peace of God Dr. DeHaan found for himself in Jesus Christ and which he had sought so fervently to bring to his listeners.

The cemetery plot had been hurriedly purchased after the Doctor's death; he never quite believed that he would leave the world by the route of the undertaker. He had often said though, if he did die, he hoped to be buried near someone who held theological views differing with his concerning the imminent, pretribulation rapture of the Church. "Then I can say as we are caught up to be with the Lord, 'I told you so'!" he would quip with his half smile. Then, "But I probably wouldn't really do that, for God says we'll all be changed in the twinkling of an eye."

Ironically, his grave is next to that of Bernard ("Bernie") Zondervan, the man who, with his brother "Pat," had published Dr. DeHaan's books and who was a member of the Christian Reformed Church, noted for its amillennialism.

The grave site in Woodlawn Cemetery, is perhaps a quarter of a mile crow's flight from the office of the Radio Bible Class and situated on a shaded green slope where squirrels play and build their nests in the trees. Just to the west of the grave a few yards are three water oaks growing from the same base, and on certain days when gentle breezes rustle the leaves some who knew the Doctor well can almost hear a familiar, much loved sandpapery voice giving a profound object lesson on the Trinity. The simple granite gravestone, guarded by a gnarled, moss-streaked silver maple, eloquently testifies of that great truth which M. R. DeHaan so keenly believed and fervently broadcast around the world:

... THE LORD HIMSELF SHALL DESCEND FROM HEAVEN ...
AND THE DEAD IN CHRIST SHALL RISE ... 1 THESS. 4:16

PERHAPS TODAY

Epilogue

In the weeks following his father's death, letters poured in from faithful listeners assuring Richard DeHaan that they were praying for him. Their overwhelming vote of confidence made him realize just how wonderfully Joshua 1:5 was being worked out by God in his life: "As I was with Moses, so I will be with thee: I will not fail thee, nor forsake thee. Be strong and of a good courage. . . ."

Today, as he continues enthusiastically teaching the Radio Bible Class, Richard DeHaan is unique among Gospel broadcasters. He is the only son of a famous radio preacher to carry on his father's work.

Under the leadership of Richard, God has strengthened the outreach of the Radio Bible Class ministry. New stations have been added.

In 1968 a television ministry was begun. It was a move with deep roots.

During Dr. DeHaan's lifetime, as television became popular, his associates remarked on several occasions that the Doctor would be a tremendous TV personality. People liked him on the radio, they reminded him, and liked him even better when they saw and heard him in person.

"I'm not the man for television," DeHaan once told Richard in all humility. "The Lord gave me radio, and

He has blessed it far beyond all I could have dreamed. But, Richard, if you want to go on television, fine!"

Reflecting on the comment, Richard believes God led his father in this decision. "He just couldn't have taken it with his heart — both on radio and television. It is so different from radio. He would have had a premature death, humanly speaking."

The fall 1968 launching of the Radio Bible Class telecast, "Day of Discovery," grew out of much prayer and planning on the part of all key RBC personnel. Though Grand Rapids remains headquarters city for the Radio Bible Class, the telecast originates in the Bayfront Center Auditorium in St. Petersburg, Florida. Here many friends of Radio Bible Class and tourists from much of the United States come to be part of the telecast.

Thus the vibrant, God-given message of the Radio Bible Class reaches out in a greater degree than ever. Through radio, literature and television, the ministry begun by M. R. DeHaan goes on and continues to expand. And because of this increasing outreach, a growing number of faithful Class members heed the closing words of the broadcast, "Keep on praying, working, and watching!"